teach®
yourself

how to get on a tv show

how to get on a tv show
katherine lapworth

Launched in 1938, the **teach yourself** series grew rapidly in response to the world's wartime needs. Loved and trusted by over 50 million readers, the series has continued to respond to society's changing interests and passions and now, 70 years on, includes over 500 titles, from Arabic and Beekeeping to Yoga and Zulu. What would you like to learn?

be where you want to be with **teach yourself**

For UK order enquiries: please contact Bookpoint Ltd, 130 Milton Park, Abingdon, Oxon OX14 4SB. Telephone: +44 (0) 1235 827720. Fax: +44 (0) 1235 400454. Lines are open 09.00–17.00, Monday to Saturday, with a 24-hour message answering service. Details about our titles and how to order are available at www.teachyourself.co.uk

For USA order enquiries: please contact McGraw-Hill Customer Services, PO Box 545, Blacklick, OH 43004-0545, USA. Telephone: 1-800-722-4726. Fax: 1-614-755-5645.

For Canada order enquiries: please contact McGraw-Hill Ryerson Ltd, 300 Water St, Whitby, Ontario L1N 9B6, Canada. Telephone: 905 430 5000. Fax: 905 430 5020.

Long renowned as the authoritative source for self-guided learning – with more than 50 million copies sold worldwide – the **teach yourself** series includes over 500 titles in the fields of languages, crafts, hobbies, business, computing and education.

British Library Cataloguing in Publication Data: a catalogue record for this title is available from the British Library.

Library of Congress Catalog Card Number: on file.

First published in UK 2008 by Hodder Education, part of Hachette Livre UK, 338 Euston Road, London, NW1 3BH.

First published in US 2008 by The McGraw-Hill Companies, Inc.

This edition published 2008.

The **teach yourself** name is a registered trade mark of Hodder Headline.

Typeset by Transet Limited, Coventry, England.
Printed in Great Britain for Hodder Education, an Hachette Livre UK Company, 338 Euston Road, London NW1 3BH, by CPI Cox & Wyman, Reading, Berkshire RG1 8EX.

The publisher has used its best endeavours to ensure that the URLs for external websites referred to in this book are correct and active at the time of going to press. However, the publisher and the author have no responsibility for the websites and can make no guarantee that a site will remain live or that the content will remain relevant, decent or appropriate.

Hachette Livre UK's policy is to use papers that are natural, renewable and recyclable products and made from wood grown in sustainable forests. The logging and manufacturing processes are expected to conform to the environmental regulations of the country of origin.

Impression number   10 9 8 7 6 5 4 3 2 1
Year   2012 2011 2010 2009 2008

contents

acknowledgements

I would like to thank Maverick TV and Hodder Education for giving me the chance to delve into the world of the television contributor and write this book.

Everyone I interviewed gave their time, tips and, in many cases, their contacts willingly and were all enormously entertaining to talk to and I thank them for that. In particular, I am extremely grateful to Julie Jones for rounding up numerous contributors when I needed them and being so helpful, no matter what I asked for; and Carolyn Phillips for giving me the time and space to do the research and the writing.

Finally, thanks should go to my mother who made me enter a writing competition in *The Birmingham Post* at the age of 7 which ultimately led to my first ever television appearance – on *Tinger & Tucker*. There have been a couple more TV appearances since then but none so nerve-wracking, baffling and downright entertaining as sitting alongside Aunty Jean and an assorted collection of puppets.

01

which programme?

In this chapter you will learn:
- which programme is best for you
- the different kinds of programme available
- where to find information on programmes
- what to do if your favourite programme isn't advertising.

If you read a lot of books, you're considered well-read.
But if you watch a lot of TV, you're not considered
well-viewed.

(Lily Tomlin, actress)

How many times have you watched a programme at home and thought, 'That looks like fun, I'd love to do that'? And then you've turned the channel over and forgotten all about it because you weren't sure how to go about it or what the programmes were looking for. Just how *do* you get yourself on television?

Being on television is exciting. It is a chance to step out of your normal life and feel like a celebrity. You become the centre of attention, sometimes the focus for a whole programme. There are opportunities to: win prizes; get a new body; revamp your relationship, garden or house; travel the world and meet extraordinary people; perhaps to become famous – or just have 15 minutes of TV time and a really great experience.

This book looks at how you can appear on television; that is how to appear as *you*, not as a professional presenter, a sportsman/woman or actor. And for that, we need programmes that feature Joe Public as their stars.

You will see a lot of different descriptions bandied about to describe these kinds of programme: 'observational documentary', 'factual entertainment', 'entertainment documentaries', 'features documentary' – even the programme makers do not always agree on one description over another. However, there is one description that will suit us for the purposes of this book – 'reality' television. In other words, television programmes that are not news, dramas, nature documentaries or sports. That leaves a huge variety of shows that come under the 'reality' label and they make up a substantial – and popular – part of the television schedules.

Reality television covers anything from quizzes to makeovers, talent to talk shows. The age of reality television really took off around 2000 but it is not a new phenomena. Perhaps the first reality show in the world was *Candid Camera* in America. First broadcast in 1948, it showed unsuspecting members of the public being the victims of pranks. From that point on, television began to realise the value of having 'ordinary' people appear as the star in programmes. Even Hollywood has picked up on the reality genre. *The Truman Show* (1998) is a film about a man who does not realise that his life is an artificially-constructed reality soap opera, being televised 24 hours a day and broadcast round the world.

'The popularity of reality TV has grown. I think that's because there was a time when TV programmes became formulaic and predictable. Reality TV showed people doing real, shocking things. In addition to this, we like to see people succeed; we enjoy watching the underdog triumph and that's what you can get in a reality programme.'

(Riaz Patel, executive producer of *How To Look Good Naked*, *Ultimates*, *Why Can't I Be You?* and *Into Character*)

'Reality has kicked off big time lately. I believe it's related to the public's want to see programmes like this. If [the public] don't watch these programmes, they don't get commissioned again. We all like to watch people under pressure – whether they're famous or "ordinary folks".'

(Kirsty Lord, assistant producer of *10 Years Younger*)

Do it for the right reasons

Don't do it because:

- you would like something for free
- you've got a couple of hours to spare
- you're desperate to appear on a TV programme – any programme
- you really, *really* need the prize money
- you just want to become rich and famous.

Do it because:

- you'd like to have some fun
- there is something you really would like to change
- you would like to see how TV programmes are made
- you have an expertise or knowledge that you would like to share with others
- you want to be part of a challenging and creative process.

Television has to be something you really want to do, for all the right reasons. Aiming to get onto a programme so you can have a free trip to another country or a new outfit on someone else's expense is just not good enough. Neither is trying to get onto a property programme, despite having no desire to move house, just so you can have a look around other people's homes. You really need to have genuine reasons to want to be on television. And yes, a genuine reason can be that you just want to have a bit of fun. Some programmes are ideal for that, such as quiz or game shows, while the content and success of other reality programmes is all about a deep-rooted desire to change or achieve something, like successfully meeting a challenge.

There has to be some integrity, from both the contributor (or 'the subject' as they are called in the US) and the production team, to make a show successful and watchable. Not only are the casting producers and researchers very good at spotting 'wannabes', rather than genuine people with real reasons for appearing, but the viewing public can pick out a fraud just as easily. Ultimately, that doesn't make for an enjoyable programme.

> 'You need to have something that producers want ... such as yourself, or your house, or your pet or your illness. Most people who think they'll be good on television aren't. Ask your friends to tell you what they think. What do you want to get out of it? For example, on *10 Years Younger* people have to genuinely want to look younger, rather than just appear on television for the sake of it. But there will be a programme out there for everyone.'
>
> (Mark Downie, executive producer of *Embarrassing Illnesses*; former commissioning editor, Channel 4 daytime – responsible for commissioning *Deal Or No Deal*)

Be prepared

Television is a great experience if you enjoy being part of a team. True, it involves hard work, long hours and, frankly sometimes it can all be a bit confusing. But it can also be a very rewarding, enjoyable and creative process for everyone involved, with the added bonus that you are being watched by and entertaining millions of people at home.

Now this may be stating the obvious but being 'in' a programme is very different from watching it from the comfort and safety of your living room. Your favourite programme will feel completely different when you are in front of the camera with the red recording light winking at you and a hushed studio hanging on your every word. So, if your ambition is to be on a particular programme, you must start to think about it in quite a different way – not as a viewer, but as a potential contributor.

A good source of background information is readily available to you. Many programmes have large, official websites where you can:

- be taken on a 'behind-the-scenes' tour
- join a 'forum' and become part of the community so you take part in discussions
- find out about current contributors/judges/celebrities
- get the latest news.

This may sound even more obvious, but it really is a good idea to *watch* television programmes, especially the shows that you are interested in appearing on as a contributor or subject. That means concentrating on what is going on in the programme, rather than letting it wash over you as a bit of entertainment. If you do this you will learn:

- about the kind of people the programme makers are looking for – would you fit in?
- how they make the programme – do you like what the contributors have to do?
- how they treat people – do you like what you see?

Record the programmes that you are interested in, so that you can study them a few times. This will help you to:

- study the structure and pattern of a show
- understand the kind of questions that get asked
- learn how the questions are asked
- see what contributors are asked to do
- get to know how the contributors are treated.

Being part of a television programme involves commitment, concentration and energy. You have to acknowledge that a camera crew is going to step into your life and start recording. And, depending on the programme, this can mean recording your highs and lows, your views and your prejudices, on tape for posterity. Emotions and opinions are golden moments for programme makers and the stronger they are expressed, the better. These moments can lift a programme, making it more watchable and memorable for the viewer.

It is not that programme makers will deliberately try to catch you out, or make you say or do something for added effect; but they will not necessarily turn the camera off if you do get a bit weepy, over the top or even downright controversial. The crew are there to do a job and make a programme; they are not likely to take you to one side and give you pointers on how to behave or what your opinions should be.

Before becoming involved in a programme, prepare yourself by thinking long and hard about what you might be getting into and whether it's what you really want. The great viewing public loves to see people 'warts and all'. It can be a bit of a gamble at times, but characters who show their frailties and their strengths, usually in unscripted moments, not only make a programme worth watching but sometimes get elevated to celebrity status.

> If there is a camera anywhere near you, assume it is on and recording everything you say and do.

> 'Most people go to work in television because it's a fun, creative industry. When we make programmes, we hope that it will be enjoyable for the contributors as well. Although they are working and they're being professional, production teams are trying to enjoy themselves too. If a crew is enjoying themselves whilst they work, then everyone else – contributors included – has a good experience too.'
>
> (Jim Sayer, managing director, Maverick TV – producers of *10 Years Younger*, *How To Look Good Naked*, *Embarrassing Illnesses* and *The Shooting Party*)

The types of reality shows available

So what exactly is available to people who want to appear in reality shows? It isn't the easiest job to sub-divide the categories of programme. You could argue that a particular show can belong in two or more completely different categories: is *Big Brother* a game show (there is, after all, a prize at the end of it), a lifestyle programme or a docu-soap? Or is it all three? Is *Cash in the Attic* part game show and part lifestyle/makeover show? You decide.

With television production being such a competitive industry, producers are very good at taking the bones of a successful programme and developing the idea by adapting it to make something different but with echoes of the original show.

The following list is not an exhaustive one, by any means, but it should give you an idea of the different styles within the reality TV genre.

Lifestyle and makeover programmes

'You must acknowledge that a camera crew is going to be in your life for quite some time. *House Doctor*, for example, was an intense, immense rollercoaster ride of an experience. It was a 13-day shoot, with eight days on location. In *Grand Designs* or *Property Ladder*, you're following people's progress. The contributors have to take on board that television will be dipping in and out of their lives. It's one thing to be on television once and another to have it for a longer time – it takes commitment and energy. We deal with people who go through a cathartic, emotional journey. They're excited but apprehensive at the start. Then they plummet into despair somewhere in the middle, finishing up with apprehension and euphoria at the end.'

(Andrew Anderson, executive producer of *Property Ladder*, *House Doctor*, *Families Behaving Badly* and *10 Years Younger*)

Lifestyle is an umbrella term to describe a large number of programmes which include subjects as diverse as:

- property (*Location, Location, Location, My House Is Worth What?, Trading Spaces, Flip That House, Move This House, Moving Up*)
- pets (*Dog Borstal, It's Me Or The Dog, The Dog Whisperer*)
- relationships (*How To Have Sex After Marriage, Strictest Parents, Matched In Manhattan*)
- families (*Sex With Mum & Dad, Supernanny*)
- gardens *(Open Gardens)*.

In the first instance, a makeover is all about changing your appearance: *What Not To Wear* and *How To Look Good Naked* are good examples of makeover programmes. But producers have developed this idea further and makeovers can now involve:

- plastic surgery (*10 Years Younger, Extreme Makeover, Big Medicine*)
- your car (*Pimp My Ride, Trick It Out*)
- your possessions (*Cash In The Attic, Splitsville*)
- your garden (*Ground Force, Garden Invaders, Garden ER, Ground Breakers*)
- your home (*60 Minute Makeover, How Clean Is Your House?, Changing Rooms, Extreme Makeover: Home Edition, Sell This House, It Takes A Thief*)
- your body (*You Are What You Eat, Honey I'm Killing The Kids, Shaq's Big Challenge*)
- your image (*How To Look Good Naked, Queer Eye For The Straight Guy*)
- morality (*Hugh's Chicken Run, Jamie's School Dinners, Secret Millionaire*).

Talk shows

These shows see people come together, usually in a studio, to discuss a variety of topics put forward by the talk show host. Some programmes have a panel of 'experts'; others use the audience input as their main focus. They range from the entertaining (for example *Friday Night With Jonathon Ross* or *The Tonight Show With Jay Leno*) to the more tabloid and, sometimes, confrontational where family relationships, conflict and reunions form a big part of the show.

You can get on a talk show either as a member of the audience, as an expert or as a contributor. Depending on the show, and whether you are in the audience or taking part as a contributor, you should be prepared for it to turn emotional, even become traumatic. You may either be picked out by the show's host and find yourself on the receiving end of their 'wit' or, if you choose to air your confession or dilemma on national TV, you may be given a rough ride by the other contributors, audience and subsequent press coverage. This category includes shows such as the following:

- *The Jeremy Kyle Show*
- *Graham Norton*
- *Tricia*
- *The Ellen Degeneres Show*
- *Oprah*
- *Maury*

- *The Steve Wilkos Show*
- *The Tyra Banks Show.*

Did you know?

The world record for the longest TV talk show marathon is 50 hours 9 minutes, held by Sergio Galliani. He continuously interviewed and presented from 11 to 13 December 2007 on El Reto Terra in Lima, Peru.

(Source: **www.guinnessworldrecords.com**)

Quiz and game shows

'It's worth saying that if your desire is just to be on television, a quiz show is a good one to pick. Your private life isn't likely to be scrutinised as minutely for a quiz show as it may be for a reality series or documentary. Unless, of course, you decide to cheat on the show and get caught!'

(Paul Woolf, development executive)

Basically, for a quiz show people compete to win a prize, either singly or in teams. That prize can be fairly modest, from a trophy or a small cash prize, up to a million pounds or dollars if you are lucky.

Examples of some well-known quiz shows are:

- *Eggheads*
- *The Weakest Link*
- *Who Wants To Be A Millionaire?*
- *Dirty Money*
- *Jeopardy.*

Closely related to quiz shows, the game show format is not necessarily about answering questions to win. A game show can be about:

- bluffing (*Golden Balls, The Great Pretender, Who Dares Wins, The Mole*)
- guessing and decision-making (*Deal Or No Deal, Family Fortunes*)
- dating (*Blind Date, Streetmate, Three's A Crowd, Welcome To The Family, The Bachelor/The Bachelorette, Gay, Straight*

or *Taken, Beauty And The Geek, I Love New York, Meet or Delete*)
- food (*Ready Steady Cook, Top Chef, Dinner Takes All*)
- reality (*Shipwrecked, Ladette To Lady, Hell's Kitchen, The Real World, Wife Swap, Trading Spouses, Survivor, Lady Or A Tramp*)
- business (*Dragons' Den, The Apprentice*)
- antiques and bric-a-brac (*Bargain Hunt, Dickinson's Real Deal*)
- activity (*Gladiators, Scrapheap Challenge, The Crystal Maze, The Amazing Race, The Alaska Experiment*)
- vocabulary and numbers (*Countdown, Brainbox Challenge, $100,000 Pyramid, The Wheel Of Fortune*)
- pets (*Greatest American Dog, Groomer Has It, Dog Borstal*)
- holidays (*Here Comes The Sun, Office Holiday*).

They're not the kind of shows where you are airing your dirty laundry in public so you don't have to behave loudly or embarrass yourself on camera.

(Angela Sliman, contestant on *Deal Or No Deal*)

Did you know?

Countdown is one of the longest-running game shows in the world and was the first programme to be broadcast on Channel 4 in 1982. Originally commissioned for eight weeks, it celebrated its 4000th episode on 3 January 2006.

Talent shows

Talent shows are all about looking for hidden talent, usually starting with thousands of hopefuls who perform for judges; for many of the programmes, the public gets to vote for their favourites. Each week, somebody gets voted off. In the last four to five years, auditions for talent shows have involved huge numbers of the public. For some programmes, this is entertainment with a cast of thousands. These programmes also contain elements of game show (competition) and docu-soap (drama, conflict).

If you have a great singing voice, are good at acting, can stand pressure, whip up an amazing dish out of a mixed bag of ingredients and have that elusive 'X' factor – then this kind of show could be for you.

Popular shows in this category are:

- *Britain's Got Talent, America's Got Talent*
- *The X Factor, American Idol*
- *Fame Academy, Star Academy, Making The Band, The Next Great American Band*
- *Any Dream Will Do* (searching for a lead for *Joseph And His Amazing Technicolour Dreamcoat*), *How Do You Solve A Problem Like Maria?* (searching for a lead for *The Sound of Music*), *Grease Is The Word* (searching for leads for *Grease*), *I'd Do Anything* (searching for leads for *Oliver!*), *High School Musical: Summer Session*
- *Masterchef, Top Chef, Top Design*
- *Make Me A Supermodel, America's Next Top Model, Project Runway*
- *Your Mama Don't Dance, So You Think You Can Dance, Can You Duet.*

Documentaries and docu-soaps

Documentaries are often called 'fly-on-the-wall'. This is where the camera follows people going about their daily lives (like *Seven Up!* or *The Family)* or films them in an artificial environment (like *Frontier House, The Real World* or *Big Brother*). In most cases, although not all, the camera stands back and observes rather than forces or dictates the action. Programmes in this genre also include:

- *Body Shock*
- *The Mummy Diaries*
- *Bad Lad's Army*
- *Vanity Lair, Big Brother*
- *The Real Housewives Of New York City/Orange County*
- *COPS, The Academy*
- *The Girls Next Door, Gene Simmons Family Jewels, Jon & Kate Plus 8*
- *LA Ink*
- *Judge Judy*
- *Parking Wars.*

How to find programmes that are looking for contributors

The good news is that there are several sources, easily accessible, that advertise when and where programmes are looking for contributors.

An announcement during the end credit sequence

Otherwise known as a 'trail', this is often the easiest and cheapest way to find out if a programme is looking for new contributors. If you're keen to make an appearance on a particular show, it is always worth sitting through the end credit sequence rather than switching channels.

Wait until the end of the show to see whether they are asking for people to contact them. The programme makers will usually direct you to a website where you will find more details of what they are looking for plus how to apply, or they will give a contestant phone number.

If you think there might be a chance of a trail being broadcast, it is a good idea to make sure you record the programme so you can write down the details at leisure.

Independent production companies

In the UK, programmes that are broadcast on the various channels are no longer necessarily made by in-house production teams. The 1990 Broadcasting Act imposed a quota on terrestrial broadcasters regarding commissioning independent productions (also known as 'indies'); it states that at least 25 per cent of the channel's programmes have to be made by independent production companies.

The number of programmes on all channels, both terrestrial and satellite, made by these indies has grown rapidly. Channel 4 and Five have been the largest external commissioners in terms of hours. Five, for example, worked with around 132 different independent production companies to provide programmes aired on screen in 2005 to 2006.

In the US, there are about 360 channels of TV, cable and satellite. There are more than 20 nationwide broadcasting networks but the 'Big Four' are: ABC, CBS, NBC and Fox; with MyNetworkTV, The CW and the non-commercial PBS taking a substantial percentage of the viewing public. The networks all own production studios, which make shows both for their own network and for others; they also have off-shoot companies and subsidiaries. In addition to this, there are numerous independent production companies which provide the remainder of the programming.

With so many production companies, it is a keenly competitive and creative world. You can see which company has made a programme by watching the credits at the end of the broadcast. The very last bit of the credits will have the company logo and name prominently displayed.

You do not have to have an encyclopedic knowledge of all the independent television companies. It would be a difficult task to do anyway; there are around a thousand of them in the UK alone, from huge multi-national companies to one-man bands. However, it is worth getting to know the ones that produce the programmes you are interested in (there is a list of some of the independent production companies that produce reality television programmes in the Useful contacts section at the back of the book). You may already be familiar with some of the programmes made by independents, for example: Endemol produces *Big Brother* and *Deal Or No Deal*; Bunim-Murray produces *The Real World* and Mark Burnett Productions produces *Survivor*.

'If there are around 1000 independent production companies in the UK, then there are probably around 10,000 in the US. The number of programmes and channels in the States is overwhelming and they all have to be serviced by these companies. Many of those networks are there purely to reflect people's interests – like golf, a baseball team, gardening and so on.

Most networks in the States don't actually produce anything themselves; shows are produced by production companies. Don't bother submitting anything directly to a network because they'll just pass it on to whichever production company makes the show you're interested in. You can find out which production company makes what programme by looking through the trade press. Go to *Variety* or *Hollywood Reporter* and you'll find lists of production companies, the name of the casting director and the address of the company.'

(Riaz Patel, executive producer of *How To Look Good Naked*, *Ultimates*, *Why Can't I Be You?* and *Into Character*)

Did you know?

- By the time of high school graduation, American children will have spent more time watching television than they have in the classroom.
  (Source: *Children and Watching TV*, March 2001; American Academy of Child and Adolescent Psychiatry)
- In the UK, 56 per cent (£1.5bn) of originated output (programmes made for, and shown by, the broadcasters) was produced in-house by the broadcasters, and 44 per cent (£1.1bn) by external producers.
  (Source: *Ofcom Report* 2005)

Production company websites

The internet is invaluable if you want to get yourself on television. It will be the first place where you can actively start to look for information. If you have the name of the production company that makes the programme you are interested in, you only need to type that name (or the programme name) into a search engine to find their website.

Like any other business, the website of an independent production company will tell you a bit about the make-up of the company; who the important people are within that company, how to contact them and what the company does. In this last instance, that will mean listing the programmes they have made or currently have in production.

If the production company are looking for contributors, there will often be a link on their website to a page which gives you information on what shows need people. There you will find a bit of information about the programme, the type of person they are looking for and, usually, a downloadable application form. At the very least, you will be able to send an email, registering your interest. That is what Ricochet, the makers of *Unbreakable* and *Extreme Dreams* did when looking for people; potential contributors were asked to send in an email, explaining why they thought they would be a good candidate for the programme. Those that gave interesting replies were then contacted by the company for an interview.

On Endemol's UK website (**www.endemoluk.com**) you will find that the company is made up of a number of different 'brands' (including Cheetah Television, Initial and Brighter Pictures), which cover a variety of programmes (such as *Golden Balls* and

Deal Or No Deal) that appear on terrestrial, cable and satellite channels. Endemol takes things a step further by having an additional, separate website (**www.beonendomolshows.co.uk**) which allows you to register your interest in appearing on one of their programmes. There is also a link for people who would like to put themselves forward as an expert contributor as well as a contestant. Their US website (**www.endemolusa.tv**) is similar. It lists the programmes it makes (such as *Deal Or No Deal, Big Brother, Extreme Makeover: Home Edition*). Click on the 'Submissions' link and you can find out how to submit an idea for a show or register your interest for appearing on a show.

RDF, another large international production company and maker of programmes like *Wife Swap, Shipwrecked, Location, Location, Location, Eating With The Enemy* and *Rosemary Shrager School For Cooks* (in the UK) and *Wife Swap, How To Look Good Naked* and *Don't Forget The Lyrics* (in the US) also has links for people interested in getting on TV. In the UK, their website (**www.meontv.com**) is specifically for potential contributors, giving comprehensive information about the programmes that are currently looking for people. There is even a link you can click on if you would like to be considered for further programmes. 'If you have a story to tell but don't know what to do with it,' RDF cleverly asks, 'then get in touch with the RDF team.' So not only are they starting to line up potential contributors for future programmes, but there is the possibility that they might make a programme around your story. On their US website, there is a list of their shows and a link that takes you through to the official programme website – where you will find out more information about casting.

Twofour is another example of an indie website (**www.twofourbroadcast.com**) which has a prominent link on its home page. Go to the home page and you will see a link 'Take Part'; click on that and you are directed to all the programmes that are looking for contributors (such as *Are You Smarter Than A 10 Year Old?, The Hotel Inspector* and *Dirty Cows*). Ricochet (*Supernanny, Fat March, The Alaska Experiment*) has a 'Take Part' link on their website in the US (**www.ricochettelevision.com**) with programmes that are looking for contributors.

Practically all the independent production websites will have this kind of clear link or contact details for potential contributors (more details are in the *Useful contacts* section).

Applications can either be emailed back or filled out and sent by post.

> ### Did you know?
> The *Radio Times Guide to Film* (2007) said that Andy Warhol's film *Chelsea Girls* (1966) was 'to blame for reality television'.

Channel/network websites

You do not have to worry if you are not sure about the name of the production company or how to get in touch with them. There will also be information on the channel or network website where the programme is broadcast. For example, when the programme *Property Ladder* was looking for contributors, the posting appeared on the Channel 4 website (**www.channel4.com**) as well as the production company website (**www.talkbackthames.tv**). The Fox network (**www.fox.com**) has a 'Casting' link on its home page so you can find out what shows on the network are looking for contributors, where the open casting sessions are being held and downloadable application forms and instructions. The TLC Discovery channel home page (**www.tlc.discovery.com**) has a 'TV shows' link which will take you to the programme you are interested in. If that particular show is looking for contributors, there will be application information. For example: *Trading Spaces* asked you to email them at **Tradingspacescasting@gmail.com**, telling them why you wanted to be on the show; while *LA Ink* had a 'Be on the Show' link, asking if you wanted 'a kick-butt tattoo by the best in the biz' to apply at **www.lainkcasting.com**.

As with the independent production company websites, the channel/network websites will have a bit about the programme and the type of people they are looking for; in other words, they will specify a certain age group, background or experiences. The Style Network's *Hot Guys Who Cook* programme, for example, asked for: 'attractive, charismatic guys who are totally at home in the kitchen. If you're a Southern California resident between the ages of 23 and 40 and have a signature dish you'd like to share with the world, we want to meet you!' For the second series of Channel 4's *Come Dine With Me* (a programme about creating the perfect dining experience with a chance to win a prize) the production team were specifically looking for people in certain geographical locations: Bath, Newcastle, Oxford, Exeter, Fylde Coast and Aberdeen.

Make sure you do fit a programme's remit if you are considering applying. If they are looking for 23 to 40-year-old Californian men and you are a 45-year-old woman from Maine, don't bother to send in the application form; it will get thrown away as soon as it is picked up by a researcher or casting director.

Depending on the programme, you will either click straight to an email link to register your interest (and be sent an application form) or you can download an application form.

The following is not a comprehensive list of all the networks, cable and satellite organizations but it will give you a good idea of how to find out the information on programmes you are interested in.

UK channels

- BBC **www.bbc.co.uk/showsandtours**
  Information on booking free tickets for shows, up-and-coming events and what shows are looking for contributors.

- ITV **www.itv.com/beontv**
  Full of all the information needed for finding tickets for popular shows and a list of programmes looking for people.

- Channel 4 **www.channel4.com/microsites/T/takepart**
  Straightforward information on shows looking for contributors, tickets to shows and what's on. There is also a sub-division within this for people interested in appearing on any of the Channel 4 property programmes: **www.channel4.com/4homes/ontv/appear.html**

- Five **www.five.tv/wanttobeontv**
  This website is very clear about who it is after and for what. 'Are you a fame junkie?' it asks, 'Even if you aren't, we want you. This is your chance to help make our programmes as well as watch them.' There follows a list of shows and what they are looking for (either contributors, competitors or members of the audience).

- Living channel **www.livingtv.co.uk**
  A channel devoted to entertainment, gossip, celebrity culture and the paranormal. Any programmes looking for participants will be on the home page.

- UKTV **http://uktv.co.uk**
  This network includes Dave, UKTV Style, UKTV Food and so on. There is a link on the website, 'Be on UKTV'.

US networks

- ABC **www.abc.go.com**
  The website contains news, information and details of all the network's shows. At the bottom of the home page, click on the link 'Casting' and you'll get a list of all the shows on the network that are looking for people. There is also information on getting tickets for ABC shows.

- CBS **www.cbs.com**
  As well as information on all the shows, the CBS schedule and news, you will find a clear 'Casting Calls' link, with a list of all the shows looking for people, on the home page.

- Fox **www.fox.com**
  Click on 'Now Casting' on the home page to find out what shows are looking for contributors and where the open casting sessions are being held.

- NBC **www.nbc.com**
  Go to **www.nbc.com/casting** which has a list of all the shows that are looking for participants, the kind of people they are looking for, downloadable application forms and information on where casting calls are being held.

- Bravo **www.bravotv.com**
  If they are looking for people for any of their shows, you will find it here: **www.bravotv.com/casting**

- The CW **www.cwtv.com/**
  If a show is looking for contributors, it will be under 'Events' where you will find a link to 'Casting'. For example, when casting for the horror genre reality show, *13*, the link was **www.cwtc.com/thecw/13-casting**

- Food Network **www.foodnetwork.com**
  Go to the TV link at the top of the page and then onto the 'Be on Food' link. If any programmes are looking for contestants or audiences, you will find it here. For example, this is where *Paula's Party* will advertise for audiences for the NY-based show.

- HGTV **www.hgtv.com**
  Click on **beonhgtv.com** to find out the shows (such as *My House Is Worth What?* and *Hammer Heads*) that are looking for people to appear.

- Lifetime **www.mylifetime.com**
  The website has all the information on its reality shows, including *Gay, Straight Or Taken?*, *How To Look Good*

Naked, Your Mamma Don't Dance, Top This Party. Go to the show you are interested in and if they are casting there will be a link. Tickets for shows also have links here.

- MTV **www.mtv.com**
  Go down to the bottom of the home page and find 'Want to be on MTV?' Shows that are looking for contributors will be listed here. Alternatively, go to **www.mtv.com/ontv/castingcall**; this is the specific casting section where you can find out what shows are looking for participants or audiences.

- Style Network **www.mystyle.com**
  Click on the TV shows link on the home page and pick the show you are interested in. Details of the kind of people they are looking for and application forms can be found here. If a show is not looking for people, there will not be a 'Be on TV' link.

Official programme websites

The majority of casting call information can be found on official show websites which you source through the network websites (for example, **www.molecasting.com** and **www.duelcasting.com** were specifically sites that dealt with casting for those individual shows).

You will find official programme websites for both UK and US programmes but they are much more common in the States. Type *Supernanny* or *American Gladiator* into the search engine, for example, and you will be taken to two very comprehensive websites – with advice, information, games, competitions, shop, videos, photographs, background details, schedule details, blogs and so on all relating to the specific show. The *Supernanny* website even has dual nationality; you can click on a Union Jack flag or a Stars and Stripes for your own 'local' site.

Casting and talent websites

'Casting in TV is critical. Good contributors make good programmes – it's as simple as that. If someone is interesting and engaging then it makes our job an easy one, often the most basic of scenarios will hold your attention. Conversely, if the contributor is weak on screen, then we can end up having to use every trick we've got in order to make the show a good watch – exciting editing, dynamic visuals and, of course, a good dollop of music can go a long way towards disguising a so-so performance.

In my experience, the casting agency websites really do work. I'm not 100 per cent in favour of them because I don't think that all the people that apply through them are necessarily doing so for the right reasons. They may just be desperate to get on TV, or be looking for some kind of freebie; they may often twist their applications to make them sound like they're just what the production company are looking for. We tend to pick up on that, but sometimes not before they've gone through a stage or two.

Having said that, they can often be very useful. We produced a series for Five called *How To Have Sex After Marriage*. It came as no surprise that finding contributors prepared to be open about the state of their marriage and expose the intimate details of their love life wasn't easy. We tried the usual ways: stopping people on the street, phoning pubs and clubs, restaurants, hairdressers, leisure centres, anywhere people meet. We had thousands of flyers printed up and distributed, all with very little success. In the end I would guess that up to 70 per cent of our eventual contributors were found through these website agencies. So yes, in this instance, the website agencies worked very well for us.'

(Neil Edwards, executive producer of *How To Have Sex After Marriage*, *Open Gardens*, *The Estate We're In*, *The Hotel Inspector* and *Life Begins Again*)

These casting agencies are a good place to start to look for programmes in search of contributors. Although they also act as actors', musicians', models' and extras' databases, they are an ideal place for television companies and potential contributors to find each other. They are rather like dating agencies – matching up programmes which need people with people who want to get on programmes. Producers like them because they get instant access to people who are interested in wanting to be on television.

A large number of programmes looking for contributors appear every day on these sites and they range from quizzes, dating games and documentaries to lifestyle and makeover shows and appearing as extras in dramas and movies. They are really good sites to find multiple listings of potential programmes, all in one place.

The downside is that, unlike the channel and production company websites, you sometimes have to pay a subscription to become a member. It is generally not a huge amount of money but you should take that into account if you are considering using these websites.

How they work

Casting and talent websites work using a two-pronged approach. A television company will register the details of programmes that are either in development or production.

At the same time, you can register your own details on the website (photos, statistics, contact details, any skills and previous experience). Casting directors can look through the web pages to see who they might be interested in and contact them directly.

The main agencies mentioned and used by pretty much every producer, assistant producer and researcher we spoke to are the following.

1iota (US) **www.1iota.com**	• This is an event planning, promotions and audience co-ordination website, but they also have a casting call link. • Go to 'Get exposed' and follow the link to see if there are any shows looking for people.
Beonscreen (UK/US) **www.beonscreen.com**	• This website has useful information on TV shows looking for contributors and audiences in the UK, US and Germany. There are also details on TV jobs and numerous resources (TV- and film-related books; courses; competitions; showbiz news). • It includes casting call information on reality TV, documentaries, entertainment, quiz shows. • You must be at least 16 to register as a member. • Membership is either standard (free) or gold (a one-off, lifetime payment of £19.99/$39.99).

Members can post their details, receive email messages and apply to postings.

- Gold members can upload a photo with their profile, receive emails about casting calls before standard members and be put top of any database search conducted by the production companies.
- Also, it has other websites which link into the main one (for example, **www.beonlive.com** for TV programmes and **www.beonpaper.com** for newspapers and magazines looking for contributors).

The Casting Suite (UK)
www.thecastingsuite.co.uk

- This is predominantly a talent agency for extras.
- It costs around £77 to join for a year; they do not charge commission.
- The annual charge covers the cost of setting up your own web page which shows your profile, photos and show reel which is shot in The Casting Suite's own studios.
- Photos are taken for free, but there is a charge for the show reel.
- The website features opportunities to work in some reality TV programmes, photo shoots, music videos, adverts and films.

Hollywood Northern
Entertainment (US)
**www.hollywoodnorth
entertainment.com**

- You sign up with this agency by filling in an email with your contact details, hobbies, likes/dislikes and the shows you are interested in.
- The agency then puts forward candidates to casting directors.
- They concentrate solely on casting people for reality TV shows.

Islandoo (UK) **www.islandoo.com**	• Originally launched to audition people for Channel 4's *Shipwrecked*, the website has opened up their casting system. • Islandoo is completely free. You do not have to pay to have your details seen by anyone. • You can apply for as many 'fame' opportunities as you like. • It also doubles up as a social networking site. • It is predominantly aimed at 18 to 25-year-olds.
Make Me Famous (UK) **www.makemefamous.tv**	• The site has free access and uploading. • You register on the site and upload a photo and brief description of yourself. • The list of available auditions is constantly updated. • The categories listed are: singers/musicians, actors, dancers, models, presenters and reality TV.
Reality TV Casting (US) **www.reality-tv-casting.com**	• This agency offers information on reality TV castings by email (free) and enables you to search for reality TV shows and auditions (free). • You have to register to read the casting information in full. • You have to submit your email and contact information for the shows you are interested in, and casting reps will respond if you are right for their show.
Reality TV Casting Call (US) **www.realitytvcasting call.com**	• This site is not affiliated to any of the shows, so do not send in headshots or application forms. • Register to receive a free email newsletter and get sent the latest casting calls for free.

Reality Wanted (US)
www.realitywanted.com

- Casting directors can post their casting calls on this website.
- Use this website to apply to and get cast in reality TV shows.
- This is a free service, but there are upgradeable membership packages.
- You create your own profile on the website and you can upload photos.
- The site is also used by casting professionals who can post free casting call notices.

StarNow (UK/US)
www.starnow.co.uk or
www.starnow.com

- From the homepage, click on the country link that you are interested in. There are country listings for: Australia, Canada, Ireland, New Zealand, South Africa, the UK and the USA.
- The website offers a service to TV companies, advertising agencies, theatres and event promoters to place classified ads online.
- It also has an online 'talent community' which allows you to create your own profile, with photos and video/MP3 files.
- It is free to register and receive casting call emails.
- If you want to apply for a casting call or have the advertisers contact you directly, you will need to subscribe to the service; you can start with just one month's membership. Costs are around £10.99/$9.99 for one month; £6.99/$5.99 a month for three months' membership or £4.99/$4.99 a month for six months' membership. They do not charge any commission.
- You have to be over 18 to apply, although a parent or guardian can

submit your profile on your behalf.

- Casting call information is regularly posted on: reality TV; audiences wanted; actors and extras (as well as work for and profiles of models, dancers, photographers).

Star Search and Elite Casting (US)
www.starsearchcasting.com
www.elitecastingnetwork.com

- These are large online casting sites for models, performers, extras, entertainers and people wanting to be on reality TV. They also post requests for locations, cars, animals, and so on.
- There is no age limit, although children under 18 must get the permission of their parents to join.
- Membership is free but there are five different membership levels: bronze – free; silver – $9.95 a month or $99.95 a year; gold – $14.95 a month or $124.95 a year; platinum – $19.95 a month or $174.95 a year; diamond – $24.95 a month or $199.95 a year.
- The 'higher' the membership, the more you get for your money. For example: bronze membership gives you one photo and a full biography; diamond membership gets you the highest ranking in talent searches – 100 photos on your personal profile, web addresses, the facility to attach documents such as audio and video files, plus 100 free SMS credits.

To Be Seen (UK)
www.tobeseen.co.uk

- Registered members can create a profile, along with up to three photos, and can apply for any of the jobs listed on the website.
- Job opportunities are advertised for reality TV participants, presenters, actors, extras, models,

dancers and musicians.
- Casting directors and producers also advertise on the website.
- Registered members must be 18 years old; minors need to obtain the consent of a parent or guardian. At the time of going to print, To Be Seen was not taking members under the age of 16.
- You can either pay (£9.50) on a rolling month-by-month basis or a yearly subscription of £55.

Don't expect to see every programme that is looking for contributors advertised on these websites. For some programmes, producers are looking for completely fresh faces, people who were not actively seeking to appear on a programme in the first place. In some instances, television makers can be slightly suspicious of people who are eager to be contributors on their programmes. Do they just want to go on TV for the sake of it, rather than to help them make a brilliant programme, or are they genuinely interested in being part of the whole production process?

Other websites

TV producers will also target specific websites to advertise certain types of show. Dating websites are popular with production teams of programmes such as *Meet You At The Altar* because they are aimed at the 18 to 34 age group, who tend to be the core group for such programmes. Other websites that will feature adverts for potential contributors are ones that deal with living abroad and/or moving house; for instance *A Place In The Sun: Home Or Away* has often advertised on such websites. Websites about music, gigs and clubbing are another good source of information on up-and-coming programmes, specifically those aimed at (obviously) music, and websites for dog owners are good places to see adverts for badly-behaved dog programmes. You get the idea.

For the producers, the purpose is to catch the attention of people who are already interested in that particular subject or idea; they are more likely to put themselves forward and be genuinely interested in the programme's outcome.

In the USA, there are a lot of websites that are devoted to news, blogs, information and recaps on reality programmes. These are also a very good source of general information where you can gather background knowledge on your chosen programme, and include the following:

- **www.beonrealitytv.com** – a reality TV auditions blog with news of the latest casting calls and links into the programme websites and emails
- **www.craigslist.org** – information on casting calls and jobs in TV, film and entertainment
- **www.sirlinksalot.net** – includes link to 'Casting calls'
- **www.realitytvworld.com** – under 'Reality TV News', there's an 'Application News' link which takes you to a very comprehensive list of casting calls currently available
- **www.tvsquad.com** – a TV blog which sometimes gives information on casting calls
- **www.tvtracker.com** – gives information on up-and-coming TV shows, especially those that are in development; membership is by monthly subscription.

Quiz websites

Two very comprehensive sources of information on auditions for quiz shows in the UK can be found on:

- **www.quizzing.co.uk** – the website for what one quiz show researcher called 'hard-core quizzers'
- **www.howtowin.co.uk/offtv** – a guide to entering competitions, including those on satellite and terrestrial television.
- In addition, a general email for contestant enquiries for BBC-only programmes is: **entertainmentcontestant@bbc.co.uk**.

In the US there are a couple of useful websites for quiz show information:

- **www.gsn.com** (Game Show Network or GSN) – go to the GSN TV link and you will see a list of shows. Click on the one you are interested in to see if they are looking for contestants or are looking for audiences.
- **www.tvgameshows.net** (TV Game Shows) – a weekly game show magazine that also advertises casting calls. There is a link to 'Game Show Contestants needed'. Enter your email address and describe how you'd spend your winnings.

Getting through on quiz/game show phone lines can be difficult if the programme is a popular one. To maximize your chances, call at odd hours. If the phone lines are open until late (after midnight) call late at night, after the rest of the world has gone to bed. You have a better chance of getting through.

Company intranet

Production companies will often advertise on a company's intranet, looking for so-called 'ordinary people'. These obviously tend to be the larger, national companies with a substantial workforce. There is no guarantee that an advert will appear or when it will appear. It's just a case of keeping your eyes open.

Magazines

Look out for adverts in television magazines and guides or their online equivalents, such as: *Radio Times, TV & Satellite Week, TV Quick, TV Choice, What's On TV, TV Times, TV Easy, Entertainment Weekly, TV Guide.* They are a popular source for some of the production companies. *Backstage East* and *Backstage West* are publications in the US for actors but they also include information on casting calls for reality TV (**www.backstage.com** is the online publication).

Some programmes in the UK, like *Grand Designs, A Place In The Sun* and *Countryfile* have magazines that accompany the show. If you subscribe to any of them, keep an eye out for requests for contributors as well as articles on how programmes are produced and what they are looking for in a successful programme.

In the US the following magazine websites are a great source of information:

- **www.tvguide.com**
- **www.tv.com**
- **www.realitytvmagazine.com**

Radio stations

Radio stations, especially the local ones, are another good place for production companies to target potential contributors, especially when they are looking for a particular geographical mix for their programme.

'We've even used posters in chip shop windows. If you're working on a beauty-related programme, you can advertise in hairdressing salons and nail bars. We are always looking at ways of finding new people; for example, for *10 Years Younger* when we wanted a male contributor, we went to DIY stores. You're more likely to find one there than in a nail bar. And we still do it the old-fashioned way and go out on the street and talk to people!'

(Kirsty Lord, assistant producer of *10 Years Younger* and *Embarrassing Illnesses*)

Case study: *Tricia*

Every programme producer has very different structures for finding people. *Tricia*, for example, finds the majority of its people through the phone line after the programme: 'Leave your name/number and problem on the answer machine'. For example, if they are looking for people with problems with a family member and you have relationship issues with your father, you would leave your information and then a researcher would phone back and chat with you for about 10 to 15 minutes to find out more.

The production team on a programme like *Tricia* are also proactive and go looking for contributors. The team trawls through newspapers and tracks people down (in other words, they cold call them). Equally, if someone has done an interview with the press that the production team feels would make a good programme, they will approach the journalist to help them make contact.

They may also go out and about and vox pop people (approach people in the street and talk to them), or they will call various groups with an 'interest' in the subject (domestic violence or drinking problems for example).

Elsewhere

'The selection process changes slightly for every programme. *Big Brother* is different to any other reality show because there's a multi-level approach to finding people. If the team feels that someone with strong religious beliefs would make a good housemate, then they will target specific groups and give them the opportunity to apply ... as well as consider people from open auditions and application forms. Each year, the team reviews who they should be looking for: Should we have older or younger people? Should we have aspirational people? That sort of thing. We don't want to have the same kinds of people on each new series.'

(David Williams, commissioning editor, Channel 4)

Sometimes, programmes want to target certain specific types of people and so will advertise in carefully chosen places. *Big Brother*, for example, advertised in dance studios for one of the series; the open auditions were full of very fit men and women wearing lycra sports gear. *Wife Swap,* as well as using the agencies and channel websites, puts adverts in the local press round the country, leaflets in supermarkets and other 'family-friendly' places, such as swimming pools, nurseries and shopping centres, plus they will often contact community groups.

Researchers and casting departments will also use specialist mailing groups (such as those for statisticians or mathematicians) to target potential contributors and/or useful information.

The selection process on programmes does vary from year to year, so the type of people they look for can change from series to series and year to year. Look out for adverts in trade publications, or even in newsagents' windows. Be prepared to be approached by researchers in the following places:

- universities and colleges
- doctor's surgeries
- associations
- gyms and dance studios
- nightclubs
- shopping centres
- children's nurseries

- garden centres
- schools
- on the street.

What if you have never heard of the programme before?

It is traditionally very hard for production companies to find contributors for first series. That is understandable. No one knows what they are letting themselves in for, so TV companies have to work really hard to cast people.

It is important that if you like the sound of a brand new, unknown programme, you find out exactly what is going to be happening. You can send in an application form to register your interest, but if someone from the production company or casting department gets in touch with you, grill them about what will be required of you.

Remember that it is a new programme for the production team as well and they may be a bit unclear as to what to expect themselves. You may, in some instances, have to be ready to appear and not really know what you are getting yourself into. Just keep asking lots of questions; that way you will keep yourself informed and you are more likely to stay the course.

'Casting a new series can often be challenging – it's so much easier with an established series because potential contributors know exactly what to expect and what the tone of the show is likely to be.

The first series of *Hotel Inspector* was very tricky to cast because none of the hotel proprietors knew entirely what to expect. They were being asked to hold up their struggling businesses to scrutiny, not only by the expert presenter, but also by the viewing public – their potential customers. No matter how much you try to reassure them, it is inevitably something of a leap of faith for them. Once the first series had been transmitted, the hotel community saw the benefits of calling in the 'Hotel Inspector' and consequently casting subsequent series became much easier.'

(Neil Edwards, executive producer of *How To Have Sex After Marriage*, *Open Gardens*, *The Estate We're In*, *The Hotel Inspector* and *Life Begins Again*)

What if the programme isn't being broadcast or isn't advertising?

In the UK, if you are interested in getting involved in a programme that is currently not being broadcast or does not appear to be asking for people, you should still get in touch with the channel or the production company who make the programme.

It is not worth targeting people, like the presenter, executive or series producer, the director or the researchers or anyone whose name you might have seen on the credits at the end of the last series. People within the media tend to move around a lot. Someone who worked on one programme may have gone onto a completely different series altogether by the time that show is broadcast. The best way is to get in touch with the channel or the TV production company who make the programme and they will pass your request onto the relevant person, usually a researcher.

If you are interested in a show on American TV, you should write or contact the casting department. In the USA, production companies have specific casting departments and teams. In the UK, casting is seen as part of someone's job, such as the researcher or assistant producer, rather than a speciality all of its own. In the USA, if you send in an email or letter to the casting director whose name you have seen on the credits of a programme, saying that you are interested in appearing on TV, it is very likely that your information will be kept and filed. Casting departments have huge databases that they can access to find people for a variety of shows. So it is worth doing, *especially* if the show you're interested in is not casting at the time.

'There is a whole hierarchy of casting people; they are specialists in what they do. It's a very different skill set from other production jobs. The first step on the ladder is as a recruiter; then you become a casting associate producer, producer, then casting director. It's a self-sustainable business in the US.'

(Riaz Patel, executive producer of *How To Look Good Naked*, *Ultimates*, *Why Can't I Be You?* and *Into Character*)

Even if a production company is not currently advertising for people to appear on its show, it will be worth making an enquiry with the channel, network or production company as to when the next series is coming out. Most production companies will answer and reply with an application form. They may not be actively recruiting but they are always interested in hearing from people. Go to any production company office and somewhere, under lock and key, will be a file full of potential contributors waiting for the next series to be commissioned.

Case study: *Ready Steady Cook*

'*Ready Steady Cook* came about because my husband, Steve, thought it would make a nice Christmas present for me. He rang up the production company and asked about applying. They told him that it had to be two people and what about him? He told them he hated cooking and he wasn't that keen on the programme. "Great!" they said. "Apply anyway."

So we were sent an application form to fill in which we did together. They were pretty basic questions: Who are you? What are your hobbies? Are you interested in food? I don't feel we did or said anything amazing. We stood out, I think, because we were two ends of a spectrum. I love food and cooking and Steve doesn't.

Having sent that in, we then got a call about going for an audition. I was over the moon – scared – but over the moon. We went along and were interviewed with three or four other couples in a room at the same time. Each couple was filmed for about ten minutes each, in turn. It's amazing how people change when the camera is switched on them. Steve and I play off each other all the time and that came out on camera, I think. Steve said some really funny things too about men and women that got the researcher who was doing the filming and questions laughing. You have to have something to say when they film you.

We were told the day after the audition that we'd got through – even though they said they'd tell us in the next two weeks. We were auditioned just before Christmas and we were told we'd be filming on 26 January. So, it was three weeks between knowing we were going on and the actual day of filming.

The contract was pretty straightforward. You sign it to say that they can use the footage of you and that, sadly, you won't get any royalties! They offered us expenses to travel to the studio in Wandsworth but we live in London so we just drove there.

On the day of filming, I was nervous until I got there. And then when I saw everyone was normal – researchers, the camera crew and all the other people involved were normal – I relaxed. It can be nerve-wracking going into a new environment like a studio or being in a filmed situation. But I also told myself that this was a once-in-a-lifetime chance and to just go ahead and enjoy it whatever happened.

We turned up at 10.30 in the morning. We were met by a member of the production team who took us to the green room and then showed us round the studios. They film three shows a day so it's a busy timetable. We then had lunch while the audience were brought in. Honestly, we were made to feel so welcome. People couldn't do enough for us.

We'd been told not to wear certain things like checks, stripes or floral patterns. We could wear plainer colours but obviously not white (because the chefs are in white) or black. They told us to bring a couple of items to wear with us so there was a choice. The wardrobe woman looks at them to make sure they don't clash with the set or with what Ainsley Harriott's wearing. As to make-up, I only wear a small amount so I didn't have much put on. The wardrobe woman said I looked fine the way I was. She put powder on both me and Steve to take off the shine.

We met all the chefs beforehand. I think if the contributors don't feel relaxed, you don't get a good show so they went out of their way to make us feel relaxed. The chefs do two or three days filming at a time so they know each other really well. There was a lot of banter going on which we were part of. It makes you feel really relaxed.

The whole experience from start to finish was great. We were treated really well. Steve and I were able to take our mums with us to the filming and they were over the moon. They made them – and us – feel really special. The whole thing was totally brilliant.'

(Angela Sliman, contestant on *Ready Steady Cook*)

02

who should you appear as?

In this chapter you will learn:
- the best way to appear as yourself
- about children's programmes
- how to appear as an expert
- how to get into the audience
- how to become an extra
- about the dark side of appearing on TV.

Time has convinced me of one thing. Television is for appearing on, not looking at.

(Noel Coward (attrib))

Appearing as yourself

'There are different degrees of being on television. If one person is carrying a whole programme, it's usually because they're extraordinary or have done something extraordinary. People like this are often the subjects of documentaries and have usually been approached by a production company – rather than harbouring a desire to get themselves on television. And then, on the other hand, you have production companies that have developed a programme and now need people for it.

It's useful for us to ask ourselves the question, "Why does this person want to be on TV?" It varies enormously from programme to programme; for example, an expert, promoting their expertise or interest in a subject is very different from the man on the street who is just eager to be on television. I would be wary of someone who wants to be on TV just for the sake of it. There's always the worry that someone will exaggerate just to get on. We tend to have a radar for this sort of thing. It's not just worrying about the truthfulness of a programme, it's also not wanting to waste time on someone who won't come over to the viewer as ringing true. Viewers are very canny at spotting frauds.'

(Paul Woolf, development executive)

Talk to any producer, casting director, researcher or channel/network executive and they will tell you that *being yourself* is more important than anything else when appearing on television. They do not want wannabes, they do not want clones. They want *you*. Look at your experiences and past history, your strengths and weaknesses and let them define who you are, not who you want or pretend to be. This then becomes your character. Once you know *who* your character is, you can start selling yourself and your story to the programme professionals.

Your story does not have to be something extraordinary (climbing mountains with one hand tied behind your back, wrestling with sharks or saving whole orphanages from burning), but it must ring true. It can be quite mundane and ordinary (you've never been on a rollercoaster with your children because you are too fat, you collect milk bottles from around the world or your garden is a mess because you kill plants with a glance) but it does have to contain something that will make a researcher or producer take notice.

'Most casting directors are very savvy and trained to find truthful people. There are people who want to be on TV for a valid reason as it pertains to the specific show and there are those who just want to be on TV no matter what. And the latter will act in the way they think will get them cast. For me, 'acting' a part to get on TV is one way to be eliminated. If there's not a genuine emotional response, there's a problem. We want honesty, vulnerability.

Basically, in reality TV, there are two kinds of show: 'real' and 'not even trying to be real'. There are tons of network programmes that produce archetypes. They're looking for actors, rather than real people (shows like *Big Brother*, on networks like MTV, VH1). We live in a celebrity-obsessed culture and some people will do anything to get on TV, no matter how humiliating. We like genuine and memorable people but they have to be genuinely relatable. There is no point casting someone who is so unique the viewers have nothing in common with them.'

(Riaz Patel, executive producer of *How To Look Good Naked, Ultimates, Why Can't I Be You?* and *Into Character*)

'If contributors don't have energy, the show flags. People who know their own mind and can be real and honest are best. Very often, people are on their best behaviour and polite; it's really not necessary for television. You want to believe in the person in front of you. If you think you're really funny, don't tell me, show me.'

(Mark Downie, executive producer of *Embarrassing Illnesses*; former commissioning editor, Channel 4 daytime)

Your story also needs to be different from any other. Obviously, if you are going for a brand new show, you will have nothing to compare yourself with. But that will work to your advantage; the production team has nothing to compare you against either. If you are looking at an established programme, do not try and imitate what has gone before. *The Dog Whisperer* and *Dog Borstal* programmes deal with badly behaved or troubled dogs. If your dog is an excitable collie that only barks at men with beards but the programme has already featured the same kind of dog with the same problem, you are unlikely to get on ...

unless you can give your 'story' a different slant (maybe you are engaged to a man with a beard and the wedding is in jeopardy unless you can do something about the dog? That sort of thing). There is no point in trying to be the next Omorosa or Leona Lewis because we have already got them; the producers will be looking for someone completely different.

'People who approach us saying "I'd love to do television" can make us feel a bit suspicious of them. Believing that you're marketable for television isn't always attractive and television companies are a bit more cautious of people who approach them. I would be very wary of someone phoning me up and telling me that they'd be great on television. Lots of people have thoughts that aren't grounded in reality. Ask yourself what new thing could you bring to the screen? A unique quality is needed.'

(Chloe Nisbet, researcher on *10 Years Younger*)

Case study: the quiz show contributor

'I've been on five game shows so far. My first one was *Card Sharks*; basically it was a lifelong ambition to appear on that show. I watched it as a kid and I had always really enjoyed it. I'd done a lot of drama in high school, so I'd been used to being in front of an audience. I've always been very outgoing, so I was really up for being on the show. And it was fun. I got through the auditions, went on the show, enjoyed it and came away with $6400 in prizes.

I went on *Password* and then *Scrabble*, but I kinda bombed out there prize-wise. My *Scrabble* opponent creamed me. At the time, you could only be on three shows in a seven-year period so, at this point, I decided I wanted to go for the game shows that had cash prizes to make it worthwhile. The only one I didn't make it on was the *$100,000 Pyramid*. The reason I didn't get on there was I kept using two words when you're supposed to use one. The producers told me that if I could have cracked that they would have had me on the show. It was a learning experience. The next two shows that I successfully auditioned for were *Wheel Of Fortune* and *Hollywood Squares*. Before, the auditions all used to take place in LA. You either had to plan a trip there or live close. I was living in San Diego at the time I went for *Card Sharks* so it wasn't difficult to get there.

Nowadays, things have changed. *Deal Or No Deal*, *Who Wants To Be A Millionaire?*, *Wheel Of Fortune* ... they have travelling auditions around the States. The internet has also significantly changed things. Before, you used to call a 1-800 contestant line. Now, you just go to the game show website and check out where the next auditions are going to be held. It's so much easier now. The only downside is that most game shows are shot in LA and it's your responsibility to get yourself there (at your own expense).

Generally, casting for these shows runs along the same lines. There are a lot of hoops to jump through; typically there are three or four cuts as the casting people work their way through all the hopefuls. There are cameras on you while you're being auditioned. You go into a room of a few hundred people; you're asked a few questions; then there's a cut of auditionees; the process is repeated until there are about four or five of you left to audition for the producers.

I've had friends who've gone on *The Price Is Right*. This is where audience members are called out to take part in the programme. So the 'audition' is very quick; pretty much all they do is ask you your name and where you're from. If you can manage to have some sort of interaction with the producers, to make an impression in a very short space of time, then you've got a chance that you'll be called down.

I auditioned for *Deal Or No Deal* in Las Vegas, where I live. There were 8000 people who turned up for the auditions; it took all day. At the end, they called 120 people back – I was one of them. I put everything into it and came really close but I didn't make it.

The associate producer I auditioned for seemed really keen on my audition. In the end, though, the producers took one man and one woman from those 8000 for the show. The man worked in gaming; at that time, I worked in mortgages. I don't think I was 'Vegas' enough for the show and I think that's what tipped the balance for the producers.

I've always tried to be interesting at these auditions. They want colour – at least they do on the shows I've gone for – you don't want to be vanilla. The trick is to make yourself stand apart from the crowd. At that time, I had parents who had never flown before in their lives; so I made something of that. I'd also had a Norwegian exchange student staying with me; I said I'd use some of the prize money to go and visit him back in Norway. It's all about making an impact with the producers so they remember you.

For *Hollywood Squares*, I was the champ for three nights and I ended up with $30,000 in cash and prizes which wasn't bad. Again, I had a ball. On this occasion, I brought Whoopi Goldberg a pair of boxer shorts I'd had personalized for her. It's all part of being unique. I want people to say "Oh, he was a little quirky, a bit different." That's what gets you on TV.

You have to follow directions. I think this is a really important part of the audition process. They test you to see if you can take direction and be quick. The producers don't want someone they have to hold their hand every minute of the day. Some of these shows are shot three at a time in one day so there really isn't the luxury of time.

The actual days of filming are really hectic. You're herded around and everything's done at a really quick pace. When you watch *Wheel Of Fortune* at home, the camera is focused on one thing so that's what you're focused on too. When you're in the studio, you don't have that focus. There are a million things going on around you: Vanna White's doing her thing, Pat Sajak is doing his thing; you're looking at the wheel, the board, the camera, the audience … You're not focused on one thing and that can be hard.

Some people get freaked out in situations like that. It doesn't bother me in the least. If you have that kind of make-up (you don't get stage fright, you don't freeze), if you're self-assured and not at all timid, then you will be fine.

I think I've got the right mix. I'm obviously doing something right and I'm keen to do more because I enjoy it – I'm a game player!'

(Jeff Jacobson, contributor to *Card Sharks*, *Scrabble*, *Password*, *Wheel of Fortune* and *Hollywood Squares*)

Appearing on a children's programme

It is worth mentioning children's television programmes at this point. There is no great difference between the way children get themselves on television to adults or how the selection process works. The only big difference is that the contributors are usually between 10 and 13 years old (although some programmes, such as *Kid Nation*, will use children as young as 8 and as old as 15 or 16) and that they need to get their parent's permission to appear. (NB Some American states will require parental/legal guardian consent if you are under 19 or 21.)

Some programmes will target drama and stage schools first because they can be sure of getting children who are able to perform and entertain; while others do not want the performing type and are looking for the 'more regular kid next door' as one producer put it.

Children's programmes looking for contributors will advertise in several ways:

- after the programme has gone out
- a short film on the channel
- on the channel website (such as CBBC, 4Kids TV, CBS)
- on the production company website
- posters sent to schools
- 'child-friendly' places like leisure centres, swimming pools, and so on.

It is worth bearing in mind that many of the programmes require their contributors to be away from home; sometimes for several weeks. For example: the audition application form for the BBC1 show, *I'd Do Anything*, explained that the potential Olivers would need to go down to London from Wednesday to Sunday of every week between March and May and that parents would not be needed because the boys would be looked after by licensed chaperones; *Endurance*, on the Discovery Kids cable network, was shot over three weeks during the summer in places like Hawaii, Mexico and Fiji. Children will have to be able to cope with being away from their family and be able to get on with other children. It is a little bit like going away to boarding school or summer camp – this should be a consideration for any child wanting to take part and their parents.

> If you would like your child to take part in a television programme, make sure it is something they want to do as well. Don't let your enthusiasm for the idea of seeing your child on national television blind you to the fact that it might not be something they are keen on.

If filming takes place during term-time, children still have to be educated. In the UK, the programme makers are legally obliged to provide three hours of tuition a day. If children are required for filming during term time, they will have to get the agreement of their school. The production company can help by talking to the schools and Local Education Authorities but parents will also have to make sure that the school is happy for the child to be taken out of school. Some programmes may ask that you bring permission from your school when you attend auditions. If the programme takes place during the school holidays, then no lessons or permission from the school are required.

In the States, the regulations governing the number and span of hours a child can work each day on a TV production will vary from state to state. For the first series of *Kid Nation*, the programme was shot in New Mexico. The producers had declared the set a summer camp rather than a place of employment so the hours that the children were filmed were longer; New Mexico has since tightened up the regulations so that can no longer apply; the state has enacted Senate Bill 175, the Film Industry Child Labor Requirements, which outline new protections for child performers, defined in the bill as 'a person employed to act or otherwise participate in the performing arts, including motion picture, theatrical, radio or television products.' These requirements are similar to California and New York laws which set the number of hours a child can legally work on set (a maximum of 18 hours during a school week and no shooting after 7p.m.), ensure the children are fed proper meals and stipulate that a teacher with proper credentials be employed on set. It is worth checking what the individual state regulations allow if your child is going to take part in a programme.

Even if children do not make it through an audition, there is always a chance that their name and details are passed on to a producer or casting department of another children's programme. Parents should be asked if they are happy for this to happen.

TwentyTwenty made *The Sorceror's Apprentice*, a 21-part series on CBBC where 14 youngsters were hand-picked to study at a magic school where they faced magic challenges and competed against each other to win the title of the Sorceror's Apprentice. TwentyTwenty first did a mass mailing to schools around the country, making sure they got a good geographical and social mix, asking for anyone who was interested to send in an application form. Having gone through the applications, they then invited potential apprentices to auditions held in major cities such as Cardiff, Glasgow, Birmingham, London, Newcastle and Manchester where they saw between 50 and 60 children at each location.

The children attended the auditions with their parents but were filmed, answering questions, on their own. Fourteen children were needed for the series but the production company had several reserves in case anyone dropped out.

Endurance – a programme similar to *Survivor* but with a teenage cast – sent out a casting call in the spring looking for 20 teenagers (ten boys and ten girls), aged between 12 and 15 years old. Potential contributors had to send in a five-minute audition tape (more than 10,000 applied from around the country for the first series). In a new twist for series five (repeated in series six), the Discovery Kids website ran a poll where viewers could vote for one boy and one girl out of six hopeful contributors.

Case study: *Raven*

'*Raven* is very specific in its age requirements; we're looking for 11 to 13-year-olds. In addition to that, you need to have a very competitive streak; you need to be eloquent and relish winning. You should be physical and confident. These are the sort of qualities that are important for us and that we're looking for in our potential warriors.

We tend not to advertise elsewhere other than the CBBC website and trails after the programme. Keep a close eye on the show you want to be on. If we aren't advertising but you're still interested, it is worth phoning the BBC and getting the address of the programme. I think it's probably better to write a letter, saying you are interested in being on the next show. We don't bin these letters; they are kept safely locked up so we can look through them when the next series is commissioned.

You should always get a reply from us; either telling you to reapply at a certain time in the future or we will send you an application form or we'll tell you where and when to look out for information on applying for the show.

Application forms differ depending on which show you're applying for but most will ask what you think about the programme. When you start to fill out your form, you will need to show an interest in that show; it's certainly something that our application form really majors on. If you like *Raven*, then apply for it.

You need to show us something about you that makes you stand out from the mainstream. All people, children included, can be interesting if you can just find out what makes them tick. We had one boy audition who was rather quiet and diffident. He eventually revealed that he was a World Champion at a martial art. That made us sit up and take notice.

Now, not everyone can be a world champion at something but you might have an interesting party trick or a particular hobby. You need to make the researcher or the producer think, "Oh, that's interesting. I'd like to know more." If you have something that you are genuine and passionate about, tell us, so we can get passionate about it too. Passion is your greatest tool because you engage with people who have passion about something. Saying you play football every Saturday and are good on your Xbox or Nintendo Wii, well, we've heard that so many times. A good question for any application for is, 'What makes you special?' Even if you don't see that on an application form, ask yourself the question – what makes you stand out from the crowd? We want to know what it is.

We get around 1500 to 2000 signed application forms which is a huge pile. That's 2000 children who've downloaded the application form, filled in the seven pages, attached a photo of themselves, got their parent's consent and sent it off. The very effort required to do all that is a good thing because it puts off children who are not totally committed. There are questions like: Are you afraid of heights? Can you swim? If you answer "Yes" to the first and "No" to the second then I'm afraid you won't get through. Several of the tasks involve doing something 30 to 40 feet up in the air or swimming through cold, deep water.

We then invite the bulk of those 2000 to open auditions in cities around the country. The children come along and we put them through their paces. We get them to play some games and we video them while we do this. We have to have their parent's permission to film them; it's not for broadcast but the law requires it of us. If you come along to the audition without your parent's signed consent allowing you to be filmed then you won't be auditioned.

Your aim here is to try and shine. But you don't have to try and be in our faces. Be passionate, insightful and intelligent. Sometimes we ask the children to invent a Raven game. You soon see who the natural leaders are but we're not necessarily looking for everyone to be a leader. Some of the less vocal children have very relevant and interesting things to say during the process; we're just as interested in them as long as they are bold enough to talk to us. There's also a two-minute chat on camera which is very quick so you need to be able to talk confidently, concisely and eloquently. We look for aspiration, camaraderie and team spirit.

Unbeknownst to them, we give all the children a score which determines whether they get invited to the next audition – which is two days on an outward bound course, a great fun thing to do – as well as forming the next stage of the process of finding the best warriors. We invite 60 to 70 or so children who are vying for around 20 places for each series. We don't run the courses, that's done by the outward bound centre staff. We are there to monitor what the children are like, how they behave, do they whinge, can they get along with their team mates? The best thing you can do is just be yourself; if you pretend you're having fun when you're not, we'll probably spot it. Don't try and be someone or something you're not.

We then sit down and pick our final line up. If you are rejected, don't be too downhearted. It might be because you're a tall, dark-haired girl from Manchester and we've got too many tall, dark-haired Mancunian girls. We want to get a mix on *Raven*. We need to be diverse and show a range of children; it's likely to attract a wider audience and can make for better competition.

Usually, we have 18 children plus stand-bys. The stand-bys are those who just fell short of final selection. If you're chosen as a stand-by, you get to come along during the filming for a week or so. You won't get filmed, unless one of the actual warriors gets ill, but it will be a very enriching experience.

Last year, the winning children for *Raven*, *The Secret Temple*, were away from home, filming for five weeks in India. We need to ask the children how they will manage being away from home for so long. The two-day outward bound audition tends to reveal those who will be homesick from those who won't; it plants the seed of doubt in those children who are not sure they will be able to cope away from the family.

Once chosen, we give our finalists as much information about the filming as possible. But we also tell them they can ring up at any time. We have a FAQ document (Can I ring home? Do I need money while I'm away? Will I have my own room? and so on). There's also a one-to-one with the parents and children a couple of weeks before filming with a programme representative to go through everything.

While they are away from home, their days are slightly longer than school days. There is, as with any TV show, a lot of waiting around (for lighting or sound to be set up, for example). But we try and keep the children busy. Legally, children have to be educated during term-time so we are obliged to give them three hours tutoring.

If you're knocked out on the Monday, you won't leave until the Saturday. That's because we like to make sure that those who have to leave do so as a small group. But, while they're waiting around, we let them do things that as warriors they weren't allowed to do: sit next to the director as he watches the camera output, hold the clapper board or the boom mike. We'll involve them as much as we can.

Afterwards, the children have to get back to the real world. The winners get a prize, albeit a small one. Everyone gets a goody bag with things from the show and a boxed set of DVDs. *Raven* has a kind of cult status; children can go on blogs and forums and talk about their experiences. It's a gentle ease down from the high of being on TV.

For me and my colleagues, the beauty of making a programme like *Raven* is threefold. It's successful because it keeps being commissioned; it's great fun being on location with the children and filming the show and it has a real impact on the children who are in it, as well as those watching. It's a kind of journey for them, not just a case of being on TV. They've dealt with things like their fears and anxieties and come out the other end. It encourages them to be braver and more fearless afterwards. It's a very fulfilling experience for all concerned, especially the producer!

(Matthew Napier, producer of *Raven*)

Appearing as an expert

'Like all production companies, we are always looking to uncover new talent – the new superstar gardener, star chef, DIY man, designer or financial whizz. Our development teams are always on the lookout for potential new expert presenters. Often the first port of call might be authors who have written on the subject. But if someone has an expertise and credibility and is keen to develop that into TV presenting, then it could be worthwhile getting in touch directly with a production company. Some kind of demo tape, however rough, would help us judge whether it is worth taking things further.

As the boundary between internet and traditional TV continues to blur, the web becomes a bigger forum for new talent. If you are broadcasting yourself, putting yourself about, you will get snapped up.'

(Neil Edwards, executive producer of *How To Have Sex After Marriage*, *Open Gardens*, *The Estate We're In*, *The Hotel Inspector* and *Life Begins Again*)

Appearing as an expert can be an ideal way to get your idea or message across. If you work for or represent a charity or a company, appearing on television gives you access to a potentially huge audience.

If you have a 'hook' then so much the better – that does the work of the producers for them. In other words, what makes you stand out as something special from all the other doctors, dentists, hairdressers, stylists, interior designers and similar experts? For *Supernanny*, Jo Frost, it was her practical, down-to-earth style and 20 years of experience that captured the viewers' imagination – both in the UK and the US. She hit British television screens in the summer of 2004 and American ones in 2005 and the programmes quickly became a hit. *Supernanny* has now gone truly international, airing in 58 territories, nearly all with Frost as *Supernanny*; the series was nominated for a People's Choice Award and Frost has since published several successful books on parenting.

At the same time, television is all about entertainment. The programme is not there solely to promote your book or your business. You have to be able to add something of value to the whole process. If you are a good guest and can entertain and inform, the promotional work will be done for you and you are more likely to get asked back.

- Watch television and see how other experts look and behave on television.
- If they were interesting and held your interest, try and work out why that was.
- Did they do anything distracting or annoying, like fidget or ramble? Take note of their negative points so that you don't copy them.
- Look at the styles and approach to interviews in different programmes (breakfast TV, daytime chat shows and so on).
- Time the slots that the experts were actually on television.

When looking for experts, production companies will target particular organizations or governing bodies. For example, if they need someone medical in a particular discipline, they would contact a support organization (for example, the British Heart Foundation or the American Foundation for the Blind). Whatever the subject, whether it is astrophysics or cake decorating, you need to get known within the world of your particular subject or interest if you want to be approached as an expert.

Almost every association, university or college press office has an experts guide; this is a list of academics who have expressed an interest in being contacted by the media. If you are interested, tell your press officer or your association that you are happy to do media interviews.

Press and media packs

Do you need a press or media pack? Academics often have an 'academic' CV with all the journals they have been published in, research they have done and so on. This is not the one to send in to a production company. You will need a 'media' CV version as well. This should include:

- your qualifications and expertise
- a *brief* list of where you have been published
- a photograph of yourself (a headshot is fine)
- details of magazine or newspaper articles
- details of previous television or radio appearances.

Remember – keep it short and to the point. Producers don't have the time to read through a whole scrapbook. Ensure you have both a paper and an electronic version of your media CV. If you post it, send it by special delivery.

Whether you use electronic or paper or both, make sure your press pack is well presented and professional looking. It needs to be a reflection of you and what you are offering.

Print media

This is a popular source of research for television people. So, getting yourself in print in some way can be useful. To get your cuttings file started, begin with your local papers. Not everyone will make the national papers first time round.

Personal website

If you have a website (and you probably will if you are offering a product or service to people) it can be used to promote yourself as a television expert. Production teams will always use the internet to check you out if they know you have one. Make sure yours is kept up-to-date. Quite a few experts also have a slot on one of the casting agency websites.

Show reel or demo tape

This does not need to be slickly edited or of broadcast quality but it should give the viewer an idea of how you appear and perform in front of the camera (or microphone if you have just done radio interviews). There is more information on producing a show reel in Chapter 03, page 80.

Endorsements

If you have letters of recommendation (from clients, TV/radio producers, a well-known person) then include them in your media pack.

Keen to do it again?

If you have already appeared on television as an expert and would quite like to do it again, you should:

- Send a thank-you note to the programme makers – it helps to make you stand out from all the rest. It is surprising how few people do this.
- Add the producer of the programme to your press release mailing list.
- If papers or magazines covered your appearance, send a copy of the story to the production company; it won't hurt and is another way of staying in touch.
- Put yourself forward as a stand-by guest.
- Build up a show-reel and a cuttings file; keep the items in it fresh. Anything that is too old (over three years) is getting out-of-date.

'So many people are media savvy nowadays. They realise that presentation is important. GMTV have got a mathematician who does science experiments. His skill is communication with enthusiasm. He has the knowledge but is able to put it over clearly with enthusiasm.'

(Mark Downie, executive producer of *Embarrassing Illnesses*; former commissioning editor, Channel 4 daytime)

In your quest to appear as an expert contributor on TV:

- Target two to three production companies and write to them.
- Show interest in the work that they do.
- Do your homework; look at their websites and watch their programmes.
- Target one at a time. If you don't get picked up by one, move onto the next one.
- If you plan to call a producer on a programme, find out when the show is being recorded (especially if it's live); there is no point calling when everyone is in the studio.

If your expertise, book, charity or business is linked to a date or event (such as Christmas or the 100th anniversary of the invention of the electric toothbrush) you need to allow a lead time of six weeks *at the very least*. If you are going to target a particular programme, find out when it is being recorded. Obviously not all programmes go out live and will have been pre-recorded well in advance. You need to be thinking quite far ahead to seize the opportunity. If you get the timing right and come up with a great suggestion, you are doing the work of the production company for them – another plus because you are more likely to get on their programme.

Useful expert sources

The following are websites and directories that production companies will often use when sourcing subject experts for future programmes. It may be worth registering your details with some of them.

- Expert Sources **www.expertsources.co.uk** (UK)

  This is a directory of experts available to the media. You have to register on the site for a fee. Standard membership is £45 for one year (£65 for two years); executive membership is £75 (£95 for two years). Executive membership gives you extras such as a promotional page, a direct weblink and an extended biography.

  College or university press offices can register their academics here and charities can also get on the directory for £25.

- Foresight News **www.foresightnews.co.uk** (UK)

  This website is a forward planning service that gives advance information on thousands of key events over the next five years and beyond. Handy if you want to look ahead and see if there is a useful 'link' to your expertise. It is aimed at journalists, PR companies, communication officers and picture editors. It is a subscription service and costs around £300 per year. You can also submit events for consideration.

- Chase's Calendar of Events
  A comprehensive reference guide (available in print form or as a CD-ROM) which lists special events, worldwide holidays and festivals, sporting events, civic observances, historic anniversaries, famous birthdays. The book and CD-ROM costs around £35/$55.

- Radio – TV Interview Report (US)
  A trade publication that goes to over 4000 radio/TV producers across the United States and Canada. Published three times each month, each issue lists between 100 and 150 authors and other spokespeople available for live and in-studio interviews. Call 1-800-553-8002 ext. 408 for free information on advertising in the report as a potential guest.

- The Yearbook of Experts **www.expertclick.com** (US)
  An ideal resource for journalists and production people to find experts. There are three levels of membership for experts: gold ($995), platinum ($1595) and titanium ($2795). The company also produce the *Talk Show Guest Directory* and the *Power Media Blue Book*. There is also a link to **www.daybook.com** where you can list news, events, press conferences and seminars that will also get picked up by journalists and media people.

- Production company websites
  It is not something that all indies do, but it is always worth checking out the programme makers' websites to see if they encourage experts to approach them. In the US, for example, Pie Town, who produce *House Hunters*, have a link on their website for real estate agents to get in touch with them for their programmes.

Case study: becoming an expert

'My first television appearance came about through my company's website (I run a professional home-staging company which is all about getting your home ready for sale by ensuring the presentation is the best it can be). We get loads of media enquiries, from researchers looking for homes and property input.

About seven years ago, I got a call from a television show asking me to do an audition for a live slot, in a programme. I had to go down to a studio and two people filmed me. They said, "Just do and say something." I was totally unprepared for it – made a right mess of it. In the end, the programme didn't go ahead. I should have said, "Never again," but I liked the idea of maybe one day being good at it so I kept accepting the offers as they came up.

I would get around five to six requests a year; some would go ahead and some not. But each time I learnt more about how television worked. I would practise in front of the mirror with an opening sentence, play a few scenarios through in my head … and it just got better. I did a piece for UKTV Style and got to see behind the scenes on location. I found that I really knew my stuff and eventually I lost all my nerves in front of the camera.

I did an audition for *Houses Behaving Badly* which was more about cleaning houses than actual property. It wasn't really my bag or what I wanted to become known for. In the end, my cleaner got that presenting job and they used my idea as the name for the show. That one I put down to experience. I get much more choosey now. When the phone call comes in, if I really like the idea, I'll pitch it to death. If not, I'm not as keen and that comes over.

I am a professional speaker as well, so I have a "speaker one sheet" (a sheet of information that effectively sums up who I am, what I am about and what my expertise is) but I am usually asked for a clip of a previous appearance or I have to go for an audition. I have done my own DVD with a production company where I do the presenting so that helps to get work. I also have a number of video clips on my website now which I will direct production companies to so they can see that I'm experienced in front of the camera. I did a television presenter's course last year which gave me experience of autocue and talk back which was really helpful.

I have now signed up to a number of websites: The Casting Suite is a good source of media opportunities in general and Starnow is another one which I've just found. I still get the most from researchers finding my business website. I have promo photos done each year and keep my online profile at The Casting Suite up-to-date. I would recommend people trying to get into television as an expert to do the same.

The fact that I was not only found, but recognised as someone who could offer something was great for my ego as well as my business! It is great to be on television because there's no exposure like it; you could never pay for that. The downside can be that the programme doesn't promote the company name (especially when it's the BBC) but it's great when you get calls and emails from people who have seen you. We always try to spin in some form of promotion in local or regional press each time I do anything – then we can mention the business.

The other downside is that it can be a lot of time out of the office with no direct business coming from it. On the plus side, as far as a personal profile and a business profile is concerned, it's great fun. I'd like to do more and hand over the day-to-day running of the business to my team. That's my next plan.

(Tina Jesson, managing director, **www.homestagers.co.uk**)

How to become and remain a TV expert:

- Be as helpful as possible. If you help the researcher or casting director, they will know you are easy to work with and you will have a better chance of being asked back.
- If you say you can, then follow through.
- Practise, rehearse. Get a friend to record you.
- Think about what you want to say beforehand.
- Offer to do it again. Producers and researchers move around all the time and they'll remember you if you were enjoyable and easy to work with.
- Don't be difficult; make their life easy.
- Don't expect too much too quickly.
- Be prepared to have to take time off from work, sometimes with no pay.
- Remember to smile and to have fun!

Appearing as part of the audience

One advantage of being in the audience is that you can actually see what goes into making a studio-based programme. That is useful if you are thinking about going onto that show at some point in the future. It is fascinating to watch how the programme is put together and you can just sit back and enjoy it unfolding in front of you. As the audience, you are very much part of the programme too; you may even get to see yourself in shot afterwards.

- Seats for shows are limited and you are admitted on a first-come, first-served basis.
- Some shows will oversubscribe to compensate for 'no shows' and to ensure there are no empty seats in the audience so arrive early, well before the doors open if you want to guarantee a seat. Most programmes advise 45 to 60 minutes before the doors open but it is not unusual for people to start turning up two to three hours before for popular shows. *The Price Is Right* audience in America is asked to check in four hours before recording starts, to allow for interviews and processing.
- Tickets are nearly always free; if the tickets are put up for sale, they become void and legal proceedings may be taken against the people involved. If you see tickets for sale and are tempted to buy them, check whether they should be free or not before you buy.
- You will be given a time to turn up at the studio – don't be late! Studio programmes are run on a tight schedule and, if you are late, you might not make it into the audience.
- In America, audience members aged 16 and over should be prepared to show a valid photo ID (driver's licence, passport, state-issued or school ID) at check-in. This is a requirement of most studio facilities and/or studio security departments.
- Be aware that a half-hour programme will not take half an hour to record; be prepared to be there for at least two to three hours, sometimes more.
- The length of recording time is due to setting up shots, retaking scenes, correcting technical problems and so on.
- The presenters and performers are there to work – not necessarily sign autographs for you. Just enjoy the experience and don't stop them from working.
- There may be drink and snack machines available but don't count on it. Only one studio in Britain (BBC TV Centre) has

a dedicated audience snack bar. If in doubt, eat before you get there. You will not be allowed to take food or drink into the studio with you.

- Few studios have on-site parking (only Pinewood has parking in the UK); many of the Californian and New York studios have parking within walking distance.
- The majority of programmes have an age limit of at least 16 to 18 years old; however there are exceptions to this when much younger children are allowed in. Details will be on the websites.
- If the show is the kind that calls people out from the audience and you are keen to be one of them – go in a group. The likelihood of one of the group members being chosen is better and groups give off a higher level of energy – another reason for being picked.
- With an advance booking for 40 to 47 persons, many Californian shows will provide free bus transportation from most areas in and around greater Los Angeles. Check with the ticket agency when you book.
- Prime-time dramas and soap operas do not usually allow audiences in the studio.
- If you want show information, directions or tickets for shows taped in the LA area, do not contact the studios. They are working television production facilities and most do not have on-lot ticketing, audience or Guest Relations Departments. All the information you need can be found on the specialist ticket provider's website. If you have questions, there is always an email address or phone number to call.

Did you know?

In the States, most network comedies start production for the new Fall TV season in late July or August and, depending on how many episodes are recorded, they can film through February and/or March. During March, April and May when the regular series shows are not being recorded, many production companies produce 'pilots'. These are the first episodes of new shows proposed for the next TV season. Hardly any shows are filmed mid-May to mid-July.

What to wear?

Dress code is usually 'comfortable'. If the audience is going to appear on screen, many programmes prefer it if they are not wearing anything with identifiable logos, large words or pictures; they can be distracting for the viewer. In America, jeans and shorts are not encouraged. Depending on the programme, you may be required to dress up more formally.

The *Tyra* show, filmed in New York, is extremely specific about what it does and does not want its audience to wear. They ask that people '... come in upscale, business, interview attire. Think classy.' As well as vetoing extreme hairstyles and logos, the show asks that people do not wear: shorts, Capri/gaucho pants; T-shirts; ripped jeans; sequins; hats; busy patterns; white/white tops/white jeans; jogging suits/velour pants; tank tops; flip flops! Whatever show you are applying for, if in doubt about the dress code, ask the ticket agency.

Where to find ticket information?

All the main channel websites, including regional television, cable and satellite, have information on being in the audiences of their shows (see the Useful contacts section at the end of the book).

In addition to this, there are some useful websites that advertise for audiences for shows. You will find tickets for the major channels/networks and all satellite and cable channels that require audiences on these websites. From time to time, tickets for pilot shows and the odd award shows or one-off events will also become available.

- **www.1iota.com** (US)

  A US ticketing website where you can register as a member and apply for free tickets to shows online.

- **www.theapplausestore.com** (UK)

  To order any of the free audience tickets online, you must first become an Applause Store Member. You have to register your details with the site once and then you are able to reserve tickets to any or all of the shows (age restrictions apply). They also have a group booking department for groups of 11 or more.

  If you become a silver, gold or platinum member (for an annual fee) you will automatically be upgraded to the Priority Pass Club. This means you will be informed of shows before everyone else and, depending on the level of membership, will receive between two and six tickets per show.

- **www.clappers-tickets.co.uk** (UK)
  Run by the former manager of Thames Television ticket office, you can get tickets for shows such as *Loose Women, Duel, Bewitched* and *The World Stands Up*.

- **www.craigslist.org** (US)
  Another good source of information; the website will put out calls for audiences for television shows in the US.

- **www.foodnetwork.com** (US)
  If you would like to be part of the audience for any Food Network show, you will find details of how to apply from the website. Only tickets obtained this way will be honoured.

- **www.lostintv.com** (UK)
  You register once, with all your details, and then you can log in and book tickets to your chosen shows. Maximum number of tickets allowed per person are usually six but, for the more popular shows, that can go down to four. You can be sent emails about up-and-coming shows.

- **www.ocatv.com** (On Camera Audiences) (US)
  For information on tickets for shows being recorded in Los Angeles and New York City.

- **www.pinewoodgroup.com/gen/TV_Show_Audiences.aspx** (UK)
  Register to become part of the audience club at Pinewood Studios for TV shows such as *The Weakest Link, Lily Allen & Friends, Let Me Entertain You* and *The IT Crowd*. Tickets are free.

- **www.sroaudiences.com** (UK)
  SRO Audiences is another popular television tickets company. They aim to make sure that the audience is tailored to suit the show by carefully building each audience profile to meet the requirements of the production.

- **www.tvrecordings.com** (UK)
  You will need to register with the site; you will then be sent details of up-and-coming shows (like *Harry Hill's TV Burp, Al Murray's Happy Hour* and *Touch Me I'm Karen Taylor*). This site claims to be the only place in the UK where you can book and print your tickets instantly online, allowing you to see what you want when you want.

- **www.tvtickets.com** (Audiences Unlimited) (US)
  The website currently represents shows that are made in the Los Angeles area; it gives a show schedule so you can see what is coming up and available. Audiences Unlimited have a stand at Universal Studios Hollywood where you can pick up free tickets for your favourite shows.

- **www.tvtix.com** (US)
  A website for tickets to live TV shows in LA. Click on the schedule to find out what shows are looking for audiences (shows like *The Price Is Right, The Tonight Show, Your Place Or Mine, Deal Or No Deal*). Tickets and directions are sent via email and should be printed off and taken with you to the studio.

- Also, the talent agencies (StarNow and beonscreen) will have up-to-date information on audiences required for various programmes.

Some American ticket agencies also look for 'seatfillers'; these are people who are needed at televised specials and award shows to make sure the audience always looks full. You have to be 18 or over to register.

Did you know?

Top Gear audience

- Recording usually starts at around 2p.m. on the Wednesday before the show is broadcast.
- Recording takes all afternoon and you will usually be able to leave the studio at around 7p.m.
- If you know the show, you will realise that the audience stands for the recording – that is potentially five hours on your feet, so be prepared for that.
- You should be over 18 years of age.
- The programme also likes to have a fair ratio of men to women in the audience. If you are booking as a group, you should have around a 50/50 male/female split.
- You can find more information on **www.bbc.co.uk/topgear/show/participate**

Did you know?

Good Morning America audience

- The programme website (**www.abcnews.go.com/GMA**) has all the information on getting into the audience.
- There is an online application form where you can register your preferred dates.
- The programme makers are always looking for interesting stories about the studio audience. There is a section in the application where you tell them 'a quirky or interesting story about yourself or your family. Please do not submit stories about anniversaries, birthdays or yearly trips. Upbeat, fun stories about weird pets, hobbies, occupations or unusual circumstances are the best.'

Appearing as an extra

> 'I've been doing extra work for 11 years. It builds up your confidence and makes you able to do camera work properly. A lot of it isn't paid but it's good experience. My useful tip? When you go along to things as an extra, don't turn anything down, don't say "no" to anything. If you do what they want, they like to use you again and again. I've taken the time off to do the extra work so why say no to some things? I'll try anything once.
>
> I've built up a really good network of friends from doing all this extra and pilot work. They come from all over England. I'll get a call from someone saying, "I'm going along to do this; do you want to come?" and if I've not got anything on I'll go and do it with them. It's good fun, especially the pilot stuff. I'll find myself running around Liverpool Street Station, shouting at a box. It's like being a big kid, like you never grew up. If you enjoy it, that's what comes over and that's what gets you on television.'
>
> (Wendie Mitchell, extra)

While dramas are not reality television, there are many opportunities for 'ordinary' people to appear in the background of a scene.

Extras, or 'supporting artists' as they are more commonly known now, work in the background of a scene. It is a wonderful way to get to see how a television programme is put together, with the added advantage that you may get a glimpse of yourself on screen when the programme is aired.

You do not have to have a professional theatre background or drama school training but some kind of drama experience, like amateur dramatics, can help – although it is not a requirement for working as an extra.

There is no minimum age requirement but if you are under 16 you will need to get the consent of your parents and they may need to accompany you to a job (NB age restrictions vary from state to state in the US).

Extras casting agencies

Most extras belong to agencies. Just type 'extras casting agencies' into a search engine (either in UK or US) and you will get lists of agencies in and around the major cities (Birmingham, London, Manchester, New York, Los Angeles, Houston, Atlanta, Chicago and so on). In the UK, the National Association of Supporting Artiste Agencies (NASAA) – website **www.nasaa.org.uk** – is a good source of reputable agencies, such as:

- **www.2020casting.com**
- **www.castingcollective.co.uk**
- **www.guysanddollscasting.com**
- **www.maddogcasting.com**
- **www.rayknight.co.uk**

In the States, the Screen Actors Guild (SAG) – website **www.sag.org** – has equally useful information for background artists, such as contract information, what money to expect and so on. At all auditions, they recommend that you remember to sign in and out using your membership identification number, not your Social Security Number, to ensure timely payment of overtime.

In America and Canada, a lot of extras work is location specific. If you live near Los Angeles, San Francisco, San Diego, New York or Toronto, there are many opportunities because so many shows shoot in those areas. Having said that, Louisiana, Florida, North Carolina, Texas, Rhode Island, Connecticut and the city of Chicago also have their fair share of TV filming. Many of the casting agencies in the major cities will have online forms for you to fill in and upload your headshots.

Most major cities in the States have at least one agency that handles extra work. If you do not live near a city with such an agency, your other option is to register with an online agency such as:

- **www.moviex.com/extras** – register online (around $10); you can be based anywhere in States. The website is primarily for movie work.
- **www.centralcasting.org** – register for around $20. One of the oldest casting agencies (1925). They don't just cast people; a recent call was for cars from the 1960s and 1970s.

Other websites with information on TV work for supporting artists are:

- **www.starnow.co.uk** and **www.starnow.com** (UK and US)
- **www.beonscreen.co.uk** and **www.beonscreen.com** (UK and US)
- **www.thecastingsuite.co.uk** (UK)
- **www.extras.co.uk** (UK)
- **www.craigslist.org** (US)
- **www.twinstalent.tv** (US) casts 'real' people for reality shows but also represents twins and multiples (quads, triplets and so on) for reality shows, commercials, TV and film

---

If you are in the Los Angeles area, one way to see if you like the work is to show up on film or TV sets and try to be an extra on 'spec' (speculation). This is by no means a guaranteed way to get work, but you might just get lucky. Arrive at the location where filming is taking place and indicate your interest in being an extra. This is where the difficulty lies; it is not easy to get close to people working on the set who may be able to help you and extras are only hired on spec if someone doesn't show up or if they have a look which interests the assistant director – but it is always worth a try. You can find out where there are TV and film sets at **www.filmla.com**.

'Why do I do it? I've a passion for it; it's like a hobby. I'm a coward about learning lines so I prefer to do this or music videos so I don't have to speak. You don't go into this to make a fortune or be famous. Although you never know what might come of it. I've definitely learnt from it. I am gaining in confidence each time.'

(Jo Kingston, film extra)

Agency charges and pay rates

Agencies charge around £30 to £80 (or around $25) registration fee – which is deductible from your first job – to put you on their books, followed by a commission of around 15 per cent on any subsequent earnings. Be wary of agencies that hold castings in hotels or ask that you pay upfront. These are more likely to be a scam.

Agencies provide a service, hence the fees. Services can be anything from posting your photo in their directory to making phone calls on your behalf to try and get you work. You can shop around amongst the agencies to see what you get for your money. Remember, it is not necessary to have an expensive photographer take a picture of you for an agency directory or have your CV/resume drawn up to what an agency says are industry standards – do not be persuaded to part with more cash.

Pay rates are set by the unions and are reviewed annually, so there is no point in trying to haggle for a better price. The rates start at around £80/$120 for a basic day's work but the amount can go up, depending on a variety of things, such as:

- whether travel expenses are paid
- doing overtime
- working at night
- doing a 'strenuous' workout
- having special skills
- having your hair cut short
- going to a costume-fitting
- providing a costume (such as evening wear or uniform)
- swimming, driving, dancing, horse-riding
- speaking dialogue
- whether you supply your own car, dog or bicycle.

Walk-ons are not the same as supporting artists. A supporting artist helps set the scene; they are in the background as part of the scenery. A walk-on is *in* the story, like a waiter in a restaurant or an assistant in a shop serving the main actors. Not surprisingly, walk-ons get more money (about £20 to £25/$50 more per day) than the supporting artist rate.

When you sign up for extra work, you need to provide a CV or resume. It is not quite the same thing as a CV/resume for a regular job. You need to let the director know what skills or talents you have – these can be pretty basic, such as driving, swimming, playing an instrument, proficiency in a sport or the ability to dance. If you can juggle and tap dance while on the high wire, so much the better, but your talents do not necessarily have to be unusual.

Your CV should also have details of your height, weight, eye and hair colour, age and, most importantly, contact details. Keep these up-to-date because the more calls you answer, the more work you will get.

Get some decent photographs (at the very least a headshot) taken for the agency or website. They need to reflect the type of person you are. If you are pitching yourself as a hippy-drop-out-come-ecowarrior-tramp, you need to show this in your photos.

The days can be long (around ten hours) and you may only get filmed for 20 minutes of that time. You have to stay on set in case you are needed again for a shot. Now and again, you will finish early and still get paid a full day's rate, which is a bonus.

Having a regular nine-to-five job and trying to work as an extra can be difficult. You will need to be flexible if you would like to pursue this; the hours are long and you can often get a call at the last minute. It is no wonder that being an extra is popular with teachers, taxi drivers, students, retired people and part-timers.

Even sitting or standing in the background, pretending to chat to each other, requires quite a bit of effort. A lot of the time you will have to mime speaking, because the director does not want to have your voice on the sound track. Whatever you talk about will need to be relevant to the scene and the period in which the drama is taking place. There are some very accomplished lip readers amongst the viewing public who can easily pick up that something is not quite right when you are chatting about your football team's latest performance while taking part in a Jane Austen ballroom scene.

While you are never going to get rich doing this, you will get well fed and watered. Your meals and drinks are free when you are on set or in the studio. Location caterers usually have an extremely good reputation. The only downside is that you may have to hang back and let the stars and the crew get to the food first.

- A lot of student filmmakers need extras. You rarely get paid for this, but it is a great way of getting experience in front of a camera and you never know where these students may end up in a few years time – Pinewood? Maybe even Hollywood?
- Be genuine – be yourself.
- Appear relaxed – you do not want the casting director to think you are going to be nervous in front of the camera.
- Be honest and don't make things up about where you have worked – you will get found out.
- Be willing to drop everything at the last minute – you often get a call at very short notice.
- Be prepared for long hours and hanging around.
- Be prepared to wear an uncomfortable costume for several hours.
- Take something to keep yourself amused while you wait.
- Don't be late – productions are very hot on punctuality and they remember if you let them down. You will get dropped from an agency if you have a problem with lateness.
- If you have to go to wardrobe, props or make-up, get there promptly; everyone works to a tight schedule.
- If you are working on location, plan for hot or cold/wet weather and take extra clothing as necessary for when you have to wait around.
- Treat it like a job – turn up on time, be polite, courteous and willing.
- Don't bother the actors for photos or autographs.
- Look like you enjoy yourself – the crews like to work with keen and enthusiastic people.

People who do this make good friends in the profession. Everyone interviewed about extra work has spoken glowingly about the camaraderie and the fun they have with their friends. You get to know each other, meet up on jobs, let each other know when work is available and travel round to jobs together.

A word of caution

'Initially the show was called *Project Marriage*. They only changed the name of the show to *How To Have Sex After Marriage* after we had finished filming. I would never have gone on to a show with a title like that had I known it up front. I went onto the show to sort out my marriage, not to talk about my sex life.

We had to go through the application form stage, also CRB checks and psychometric testing. We were given a lot of support beforehand but even so it was mentally knackering, even before we started filming. It continued afterwards – as part of our aftercare, we had ten sessions with a therapist. I am an extremely stable person but I was an emotional wreck afterwards. You live your life under a microscope.'

(Melani Spencer, contributor on *How To Have Sex After Marriage*)

Television can make something quite special out of nothing. It can be enormously good fun taking part, even life-changing for some people – but there is no getting away from the fact that it can be full of pitfalls too.

The potential dark side of being on television depends very much on the type of programme but you must consider that after you have appeared on certain TV shows, your private life may not be so private after all. Ask yourself:

- Are you prepared to have the press probe and examine your life, criticise you … and your friends and family?
- Are your family and friends happy for you to be on television?
- Are your employers supportive?

'A lot of television can be exploitative of people, rather than nurturing. To some TV people, 'producing' actually means 'manipulating'. People can be 'Frankenbited'; their words taken out of context and edited in a certain way. So I think people should be careful when they are contemplating going on TV. You should go by your instincts. Do you trust the people that are making the programme? Are they forthright and honest with you? I often have to talk people off the ledge, convince them that I'm not going to destroy their lives and their family. I'm always aware that we are not dealing with actors; these are real people.'

(Riaz Patel, executive producer of *How To Look Good Naked*, *Ultimates*, *Why Can't I Be You?* and *Into Character*)

We have all read the articles about this in newspapers and magazines; the secrets that came out, thanks to 'friends' and acquaintances. Remember those embarrassing photos or clips on YouTube and MySpace that were taken at a drunken party when you were younger? They may well surface again.

Ex-wives, former boyfriends and old school-friends have all been known to reappear with lurid stories after someone's appearance on television; while some companies have not taken kindly to their employee's appearance on TV and have 'let them go' soon after their appearance.

Even if there are no skeletons in your cupboard, are you prepared to give up the time that the application, auditioning and filming process takes? If you make it past the application form stage, you need to take time off for the interview and audition process, followed by the actual filming; even then, a 'short' piece can take a day to film.

And when you do get to the filming process, be prepared for the highs and lows of filming: finding yourself in challenging (*Unbreakable, The Amazing Race*) or humiliating situations (*The Weakest Link, Hell's Kitchen*); feeling vulnerable (*How To Look Good Naked, You Are What You Eat, Trinny And Susannah Undress*) or rejected (*America's Got Talent, The X Factor, So You Think You Can Dance?*).

'We want passion [from our contributors] but we want them to be themselves. We don't want people trying to be a celebrity. We want absolute conviction and passion.

As a viewer, you can watch a year of someone's life in one hour. In *10 Years Younger* and *Extreme Makeover*, people are actually going under the knife and having major life-threatening surgery. As a viewer, you haven't gone through that pain or risks yourself so be very aware of this when you think about going on a television programme.'

(Andrew Anderson, executive producer of *Property Ladder*, *House Doctor*, *Families Behaving Badly* and *10 Years Younger*)

Case study: *The X Factor* audition

'I went to the first audition in Birmingham. None of the judges (like Simon Cowell and Sharon Osbourne) were there. But the cameras were on and recording people waiting, doing a bit of singing or dancing as well as interviewing them. I waited for around two, two and a half hours before being sent to audition.

I was told to wait outside this room with another queue of people and that I wasn't allowed to talk at all – apparently they can hear you in the room if you do. You have to be completely quiet outside the room, so a steward person watches you all the time.

When I went into the audition room, I was told to stand on the cross in front of three judges and sing one or two of my song choices. You just get two minutes to sing a verse and a chorus. After I had sung, they didn't discuss between themselves as it was clear just one of them was in charge – this person told me that I was through to the next round of auditions.

As soon as you come out of the door of the room, they make you wait to have an interview with one of the directors of the show. It's a one-on-one interview. They ask who is with you, your plans for the next couple of months, what you want to be in the future, that sort of thing. The director asked me if I had any deep, dark secrets. My dad was dying of cancer at the time; he died two weeks later. But I said "No, I don't have any dark secrets." I think now that if I had said "Yes" and told them what was happening at home, I probably would have got through a few more stages. But I didn't want to get through on that alone, and the pain of the situation was too much at the time to talk about with a stranger.

For the second audition, you're told to wear exactly the same clothes; even the people who've come along to support you have to wear the same clothes for continuity. The second audition was awful. It was a horrible atmosphere because no one was getting through and there was an increased sense of desperation from the other people auditioning. At the first auditions, the atmosphere was completely different; it was all a bit of fun.

I went in to the same room as my first audition. There were two women judges this time. And this is the killer part. I sang two words of my song and the one woman, who was obviously the boss, turned to the other and said "No". I just kept singing as the other woman replied, "Are you sure?" You're filmed while singing and they did at least look at the camera to see how I looked. I just felt cheated because they hadn't listened to my voice, only at what I looked like on the camera.

I didn't like the whole feeling of being herded like cattle. As soon as I came out of the room, obviously feeling disappointed, the steward said, "Go and tell the X Factor pod how you feel." I said, "No thank you, I'd rather not," but he kept badgering me to go and unburden myself to the pod, not seeming to understand that I just wanted to leave. I ignored him and walked away. It makes you realise when you watch the programme that when you see people sounding off about the judges, it's not Simon Cowell and the others that they're talking about at this point – most don't even get to see them.

It also struck me that, having got through the two stages, the stewards and production staff all tell you how amazing you are to have got this far. So the really bad people, the ones who can't sing but get put through to the next stage to actually audition in front of Simon Cowell are also all told that they're amazing and wonderful to have got this far – only to be told how awful they are by the celebrities.

I've been to drama schools and done auditions where they at least let you do your monologue or whatever. That doesn't seem to be the main thing for *The X Factor*; I think they're looking for good television rather than great singers.'

(AE, *The X Factor* hopeful)

Case study: *Castaway*

'I'd had a few things sent to me, programmes, pilot work and so on; some things I've said "Yes" to, others "No". I got sent the application form for *Castaway*. I wasn't really bothered; I knew it as a programme set on an island in Scotland and I didn't really fancy that. I only filled in three pages of the ten-page application form. They got back in touch with me and asked me to complete it so I did. I would recommend to anyone that they should actually finish filling in an application form.

It's really weird. When I'm doing a job application, I really take my time. When I fill in an application for TV stuff, I write it as it comes into my head. I don't hesitate. This is me, blah, blah, blah. I suppose my personality comes over better that way.

I then got a call asking me to go for the casting. I didn't know what to expect. I've been to a few castings and, if you're part of an agency, your agency will try to tell you how to behave to get through. I don't need to be told – I've learnt from my mistakes. I just go and be myself. They had a big black screen – you couldn't see anyone, just hear this woman's voice. So I just chatted away and enjoyed myself; they had my casting tape on YouTube for ages.

I then got sent for psychiatric testing. I had to go to this hotel room where this guy was sitting. He looked like a bank manager.

I've done counselling studies so I knew a little bit about what to expect. He asked me things like, "Say three words that describe your childhood." And then he'd ask me questions about what I'd said. We also talked about how I'd feel if the media started printing things about me while I was away. I said I didn't have any skeletons in my cupboard and the people closest to me knew what I was really like so I wasn't bothered if anything got printed. I also had to fill out a booklet with questions like: "There are four people, three of them are arguing. What would you say to the quiet one?" Stuff like that.

The psychiatrist couldn't talk about the programme much but he did say, "I recommend that you look very closely into what it is all about." He was right to say that because it was a tough show with really difficult times – we only had one meal a day for weeks and weeks. People would moan about things but I just shut off a bit and thought about what I could eat and do when the programme was over. Your mind definitely starts playing tricks with you though; you'd go from highs to lows all the time. It wasn't easy. We were filmed all the time. My kids watched and said they saw rats crawling all over me while I was sleeping; there were rats everywhere. Mind you, there are so many things worse in the world than a TV programme which isn't going to last for ever. I don't see the point in getting angry or upset.

Six thousand five hundred people applied for the show. It all happened so fast after I'd sent the application form in. I had to get my passport renewed in about two hours and then we went out to New Zealand – not Scotland! I was on autopilot, it happened so quickly. It was nice to be invited. Some people knew they were going to be on the programme for six months; I couldn't have kept it secret for that long!

The production team were very careful about who they wanted. Each person on *Castaway* has their opposite. You know, same age as you but with completely different views and way of life. I've brought up my four daughters on my own and my opposite was a real 'mummy's boy' and we had some big clashes. The production team know what they're doing.

I'm definitely not the same person I was before I went out there. What I saw while I was there, being away from my children – it made me think a lot about my life. It took me right back to my childhood. I thought about my mum a lot and the kind of life we'd had when I was a child. She died in December but I've been able to cope with her death because I had all that time thinking about her. The relationship with my kids has changed too. I'm no longer just their mum; they've watched me on the programme being me, a human being, coping with what was happening. They're proud of me, so that's been a bonus.

I'd go to New Zealand or Australia tomorrow if I could. You realise that there is such a beautiful world out there. We were on a Great Barrier Island and it was like something out of *Jurassic Park*. I found myself on a beach, with pebbles 100 foot high. I felt so tiny in a world of giants – I expected a dinosaur to come round the corner at any minute! Everything was so quiet and it was such beautiful scenery. Yeah, I hope to go back.

I've done a few things as an extra since coming back: something on Eurostar that was shown to the Queen, *Big Brother's Big Mouth*, *Celebrity Get Me Out Of Here*. I was in the ladies with one girl who'd been on *Big Brother*; she was having a fit because she couldn't plug in her hair straighteners, complaining to the crew and saying, "Don't you know who I am? If I don't get what I want, I'm leaving." The crew weren't bothered if she left or stayed. They said, "You're just the same as everyone else here." One of the guys who'd been on *Castaway* with me has been complaining that no one in the media wants to know him; he thought he'd be rich and famous by now.

I'm not that bothered about becoming famous and rich. If it happens, that would be nice but I don't expect it. The *Castaway* production team weren't interested in people who wanted to be famous; they wanted personalities and people who were the opposites of each other.'

(Wendie Mitchell, extra and castaway)

03 the application process

In this chapter you will learn:
- what researchers and producers are looking for
- how you can make their lives easier
- how to increase your chances of selection
- how to fill in the application form for maximum effect.

Television is more interesting than people. If it were not, we would have people standing in the corners of our rooms.

(Alan Coren, writer)

Getting your story straight

When you go through the application process for a programme, you are assessed constantly. First by researchers or the casting department, then perhaps assistant/associate producers, followed by show runners or executive producers who then pitch the programme and, in many cases, the potential final line-up of contributors, to the broadcaster (in other words, the commissioning editor of the individual channel or network executives).

If a researcher or casting professional cannot be confident about pitching you and your story to the next level, then you are not going to get very far. People who work in television develop a sixth sense when it comes to sniffing the right – and the wrong – kind of people out. If you help that researcher or producer in their job, they will feel confident about supporting your application.

Top of the hierarchy are the network executives or commissioning editors of the channel, then the series or executive producer (called the show runner in America), assistant/associate producer (AP) with the researchers or casting professionals at the bottom, as it were. They may be lower down in the order but don't dismiss the researchers or casting professionals as insignificant beings, not worthy of much courtesy or attention. They wield a lot of power because they are the ones who can spot the potential of a good contributor and they are usually the first people to assess TV hopefuls. A big part of their job is to read people; they get to be very good judges of character. A good idea – or a good contributor – will always get put forward by a researcher/casting director.

> 'The casting director will present their favourite selections to the executive producer who will then make the choice of the final list to go before the networks. If the executive producer is established and known to the networks, then their say pretty much goes and the network will trust their choices.'
>
> (Riaz Patel, executive producer of *How To Look Good Naked*, *Ultimates*, *Why Can't I Be You?* and *Into Character*)

So what can you offer? You must always ask yourself what will you get out of the programme but it is equally important to think about *what will they get out of you*? We talked about developing your character and your story in the last chapter. Once you have decided upon your story and character, you must make sure you answer the questions on the application form (and any subsequent questions) as that person. Be consistent and don't try and reinvent yourself as somebody different halfway through the process.

The answers you put on the programme application form are extremely important. First and foremost, the casting/production team want to know a bit about you – who are you, where do you come from, what is your background story, do you offer what they are looking for? Secondly, the casting/production team are always looking ahead to the final stage – recording the programme. This is where your answers will play an important part in the programme. The information you give on the application form is crucial; during the recording and editing of the programme, it can be used to introduce you at the start of your piece, or when the action is flagging, or to use as a link between one bit of the programme and another. In some shows, they may even use the answers you gave to provoke and get a strong reaction from you.

Don't put down anything on the application form that you can't back up or believe in.

What is your journey going to be?

'We would look for someone who had made some effort with their application form. You must immediately paint yourself as a 'character'. What's going to make you stand out, what will make good TV? Ask yourself "What is my story?" It's not just about liking a show or the presenter. If you're contemplating going on a makeover show, for example, you need to be very honest with yourself about bringing your "rough" qualities to the show; it's not just about liking a show or the presenter. Then it's up to the expertise of the production company to spot a diamond in the rough.'

(Chloe Nisbet, researcher on *10 Years Younger*)

In many cases, 'going on a journey' is what makes a programme. Not literally travelling from A to B but seeing someone develop and change over the course of half an hour, an hour or a series. You can almost tell where a person's journey is going to start and end on some programmes, for example:

- *Trinny And Susannah Undress The Nation* – if the subject is a housewife who has not been out of the house for the last four years because of how she feels she looks, it is more than likely that her journey is going to involve regaining the confidence to do just that.

- *Lady Or A Tramp* – on one level you are watching young women learning to arrange flowers and prepare elegant dinner parties; on another, you watch to see if they return to their badly-behaved ways or whether the whole experience makes a positive impact on their lives.

- *How To Have Sex After Marriage* – deals with couples who are at a low point in their relationship and then shows the steps the couples take, with the help of experts, to patch up their failing relationships.

- *Supernanny* – takes a family who are having difficulty raising their children and gives them the tools and advice to restore order and harmony in the household.

In the past, discussions about the importance of following someone's journey (in the context of how a programme would develop) used to take place in the production company's offices and never made it to the final recording, but now it is very much part of the programme itself. If you are able to suggest to the producers that you have a journey to go on at this stage, you will have caught their interest straightaway.

However, not every programme is looking for people on journeys. Quiz and game shows, like *The Weakest Link, Wheel Of Fortune* or *Win My Wage* want people to have fun and be entertaining. So don't worry about trying to think of an interesting journey or major personality development as your motivation for appearing on such a programme.

Filling out the application form

'The application form for *Deal Or No Deal* was very in-depth. After the show, you realise why they ask you the questions that they do; the answers give an indication of how you're going to play the game. There's a big psychological element to it. The questions are along the lines of: What would you do if you had this sort of money? What would be a life-changing amount of money? I answered £6 million to the last question. Well, £100,000 would be nice but you'd still have to keep your job on, wouldn't you? £6 million would make a difference I think. I answered really honestly and gave the answers some thought. I told them what I thought rather than what I thought they wanted to hear.'

(Angela Sliman, contestant on *Deal Or No Deal*)

Imagine the scene: you are in an office sitting at a desk. In front of you are several thousand application forms that have arrived by post and email from people wanting to be in your next series. You have to read through all of them and pick out the ones that you think will interest your producer.

This is the reality facing many TV researchers and casting professionals. As a TV hopeful, you need to think creatively and with care about making your application form stand out from the thousands. Think of the person reading your application form as your first audience. This is the person who you have to impress and entertain so they put you onto the 'must go to next stage' pile of papers, rather than bin your application form.

First of all, read the programme requirements carefully. If a programme is looking for a particular age group, or sex, or geographical location and you do not fit them – then don't bother to send an application form in. With thousands of forms to read through, the production staff will immediately discard the ones that do not fit the brief.

'Be honest. Lying gets you nowhere. It ties you up in knots and you'll get found out in the end anyway. If you've had difficulties (drink, drugs or psychological issues) and there's an appropriate bit in the application form, then put this down. It may not form part of the ultimate problem or programme but it's best for us to know.'

(Zoe Case, researcher on *10 Years Younger* and *Embarrassing Illnesses*)

Spend time on your application form. Usually, they are easily downloaded from the programme's website or you can contact the production company and get one sent to you in the post.

- If asked about your likes and dislikes or hopes and aspirations, be honest – even if it does make you sound silly, egotistical or downright peculiar.
- Don't write answers that you think the production people want to see.
- You can handwrite or type the application form – either will do. If handwritten, make sure it is legible.
- Enthuse about your job – sell what you do; it helps to make you stand out from the crowd.
- Talk about your hobbies and past times – mention them because they flesh out your character for the researchers.
- There is no need to add an accompanying letter; the production team have a very short time to read the application forms, let alone additional letters.
- Avoid smiley faces, highlighter and doodles; they add nothing to the form and will not help you stand out (at least not in the right way).
- Keep a copy of the completed form so that you have a reminder of your answers; useful if and when someone from the programme contacts you because they like what they've read.

What is encouraging is that a dedicated team, either the casting department or the researchers, will go through every application form received – even if the post bag and email brings in tens of thousands. So your application form *will* get read.

How much should you write?

One-word answers will not get you to the top of the 'must see' list. If you are not sure about how much to write, take guidance from where the spaces have been left for you to fill out any answers. If it is a one-line space, then the programme does not need much information; if it is enough space for a paragraph, then they obviously want more.

If you really do need a bit more space, then just attach a piece of paper to the form – avoid the temptation to write a small book though; the team have so many application forms to go through that they just don't have the time to read through pages and pages of extra information.

The way in which your application form is written is a big giveaway, too. Don't worry. It does not have to be perfectly spelt or grammatically correct; split infinitives will not rule you out. But if it does not make sense, the casting team cannot take it further. The feeling is that if you cannot write your story clearly, you probably are not able to speak it either.

The importance of anecdotes and humour

Anecdotes are one of the best ways to make you stand out from other people. Don't make these stories up; if you haven't circumnavigated the globe on a unicycle then don't claim to have done it. Be honest.

Most application forms will have a space where you can recount anecdotes. Sometimes, they will need to be relevant to the programme, other times it is all about what happened to you and friends or family. One quiz show researcher still remembers an anecdote in an application form where the man had been swept out to sea in a pedalo. The subsequent story about his rescue and how it turned out was funny, memorable and ultimately got him through to the next stage (and finally onto the programme).

You do not have to be the comedian and try and crack a joke on every line but you want to show the reader that you are fun to be around and don't take yourself too seriously. The ability to laugh at yourself and the situations you find yourself in is an attractive trait in a person, especially someone prepared to go on television. Amusing, funny and quirky answers will get you noticed.

Video applications and show reels

Videos, as the first application stage, are much more common in America. You will find that a large number of programmes will ask for a short (just two minutes in some cases) video as well as or instead of an application form.

Remember that this is an audition tape; the team want to see your personality, not your video editing skills, so don't get too tied up worrying about clever mixes and seamless editing techniques.

First of all, read the instructions from the programme and follow them closely – especially regarding the format. Every programme asks for something different; anything from a VHS and VHS C to a mini-DV, Hi-8 or DVD or a combination of some or all of them. If you send in your application on a Hi-8 and you were asked for VHS or DVD, your application will get discarded straightaway.

Secondly, pay close attention to the length of the tape that they are asking for. It is never more than ten minutes but is more likely to be between three and five minutes. Stick to the time limit. With programmes receiving thousands (tens of thousands in some cases) of applications, the casting department will not indulge you if you have run over.

There are a few basic dos and don'ts for producing a video application.

- Lighting is really important so it is worth taking a bit of time to get it right. Do not film yourself in front of a window because all the viewer will see is a dark outline. Make sure you have balanced lighting either side of you and shining on you. If you don't have good lighting, use the sun to light your features.
- Do a camera test before you start to check sound levels, focus, zoom and so on.
- Check that you do not have the auto-focus feature on because that can blur your image and if the casting people cannot see you clearly, they are not going to take your application further.
- If you are shooting outside, do it in the daytime, not at night, so you can be seen clearly.
- Don't have the date stamp on when you are filming.
- Ideally, get a friend to hold the camera for you so they can check sound levels, focus and so on. They can also ensure that the top of your head isn't cut off during filming.
- Try not to get too close or too far away from the camera; about four feet is just right.
- Don't film in a noisy environment (busy road with cars, beach with waves crashing on the shore, places with people talking, planes going overhead) and turn the TV off if you are filming at home.
- Try and avoid having music on the tape (obviously difficult if you are auditioning for a dance or music show – so it is acceptable in these circumstances).
- Always start the tape by stating your name, home town and state.

- Label your tape with your contact information (name, address, telephone number, email address) and the programme you are applying for.
- Label the tape/DVD *and* the case it comes in.
- Aim the camera at eye level. If you shoot from too high a position, you will look like you have been caught on a security camera. If you shoot too low, you will end up with lots of chins which is not flattering.
- Don't just sit on the couch and talk to the camera; the casting department want to see dynamic and unique people so show them where you live, work, your hobbies and so on. This is your chance to paint a vivid picture of who you are. Be creative and have fun.
- Talk to the camera as if it is your best friend. This is no time to feel self-conscious or foolish.
- It will depend on the show, but you may be asked to send in additional information with your video application (such as a copy of your current driver's licence or government-issued ID; recent photo/s of yourself; even a copy of your current passport). Check the details on the website or flyer to find out what the casting department is expecting to receive. If anything is missing, it is unlikely that the casting department will chase it up with you – your video will get thrown out instead.
- Rewind the tape to the beginning when you have finished. As any casting professional will tell you, this is very much appreciated.

Different programmes ask you to show different sides of your personality and lifestyle – it depends on the show: *Top Chef* wants to see you cooking and plating something; *Tabitha's Salon Takeover* wants to see your salon, talk to your employees and see you cutting and styling hair; *The Mole* wants to see examples of your intellect, competitive nature, physical abilities and for you to tell them why you should be on their show; *All The Right Moves* tells you to 'feel free to let loose and dance! If you know several dance styles, here's your chance to showcase them.'

They all ask you to tell them a bit about yourself (hobbies seem to be important here – they are a good way to make you stand out from the crowd), show your uniqueness and to be creative with your tape. A tall order, but if you can pull it off you are one step closer to being on television.

Show reels

Whether you are in the US or the UK, if you are putting yourself forward as a potential expert, you will need some kind of show reel or demo tape. It does not have to be broadcast quality but it needs to give the watcher an idea of what your skills are, how you look on screen and what you are capable of.

If you do get asked to send in a tape of yourself, remember:

- use new tape/DVD (check the format with the casting people if you are not sure); it is a good idea to have different formats of your demo tape available
- introduce yourself – no longer than 30 seconds
- stand close to the camera (about four feet) so you can be seen clearly
- get to the point immediately; the production team don't have all day to sit through your tape
- make sure you can be heard; you need a quiet place to record the tape
- if you don't have to, avoid using music; music has to be cleared from the copyright holder and it will be too much trouble for the programme to do that if there is a chance that the audition tapes get broadcast
- include clips of previous appearances
- keep it fairly short; no more than five minutes (three minutes is ideal!)
- you are not an editor so don't worry about putting together a polished package; the team will be looking at you, not how well you cut from one scene to the next.

Extra information

This is not always entirely necessary for every application but if you can back up your 'character' and your story with some extra information, it can help researchers and casting departments to form a clearer picture of you.

Newspapers and magazines

If you have been featured in a newspaper or magazine and it is relevant to your application for a programme, then include a copy of the cutting (not the original).

Websites

YouTube, MySpace, FaceBook, Friendster and Bebo are some of the popular video sharing and social networking sites. If people can see you first on YouTube or something similar, it will certainly help your cause; just think of it as another strand in your media CV. It does not have to be a social networking site; you may have a website in your own right. Whatever the type, it will give the production team an idea of the kind of person you are and anything that makes the life of the production company easier is a plus for both you and them. A few of the British researchers and production teams interviewed for the book had used sites like these but it certainly wasn't something everybody was doing yet. However, all the researchers, when asked about the usefulness of social networking sites as a source of checking out potential contributors, agreed that it would probably become more popular. In the States, it is a different story. Social networking sites are popular resources for the casting departments. Chance and Real who were on *I Love New York* were discovered by VH1 producers through their MySpace pages. Some US programmes allow you to send in applications online via MySpace. The internet is not going to go away so if you have a page on a site like this, make sure it is up-to-date.

> If you get a message through MySpace, Facebook or a similar site offering you a VIP pass to a casting call, check it out carefully. If you are asked to respond to a production company's email address, then it will probably be legitimate. It is unlikely that such companies use web-based email services such as gmail or hotmail. You can check to make sure the casting call is listed on the production company website if you are not sure.

Family and friends

You may be asked what your family and friends would think of you taking part in a programme and whether anyone would be prepared to be filmed along with you. Do check with everyone before promising that they are all perfectly happy and would be delighted to be filmed before returning your form. It was fine for one of Sharon and Ozzy's children to decide not to appear in their real-life docu-soap, but it would not have been much of a programme if everyone, bar Sharon and the dogs, had decided not to take part either.

Have you been on TV before?

'If it's the right person, it won't matter if they've been on another programme.'

(Zoe Case, researcher on *10 Years Younger* and *Embarrassing Illnesses*)

This question will usually be asked by every programme. If pushed, most television people will say that they prefer new faces and it is true that they are always searching for someone fresh and different.

Having said that, being on another programme will not necessarily bar you from appearing again and, whatever the production team tell you, it is not an immediate turn off for whoever is reading the application forms. Certain shows, such as *American Idol*, will state quite clearly that contestants who made it to a certain stage in a previous series (the last 50 in the case of *American Idol*) are not eligible to apply again. However, quiz contestants, for example, are well known for doing the rounds of different shows. Other contributors who have had a second chance at appearing on TV are the following:

- Steve Brookstein, the winner of the first *The X Factor* had previously come second on ITVs *Big Big Talent Show*
- Larissa Summers appeared on the first series of *Vanity Lair;* she had already been on Living TVs *Dirty Cows* programme where she had reached the final
- Wood (Randy Richwood) was the winner of *Mr Romance* on the Oxygen Channel; he was also featured on *elimiDATE*
- Bill Rancic, first winner of *The Apprentice* (US), also auditioned for *The Bachelor*
- For series eight of *America's Next Top Model*, Tia Mowry of CW's *The Game* gave the girls an acting class.

Quite a few of the contributors interviewed for this book had appeared on at least two or three programmes; in some cases because they had been contacted directly by a production team to appear on their show.

After all, for the producers, the positive side of having someone who has appeared on television before means that they have cast someone who has the energy that got them through an application process before, beating (probably) several thousand other applicants; they then delivered in the final recording. That is quite a tempting prospect for programme makers, especially those making new programmes. They will want tried and tested contributors rather than complete unknown quantities.

But the producers will not want to see your face appearing on a different programme a week before theirs is about to be broadcast. Even the ubiquitous quiz show contestants have to wait some time between appearing on different shows. Equally, if you were applying for *10 Years Younger* and you have also appeared on *Extreme Makeover*, it is unlikely that you would get on *10 Years Younger*.

If you are keen to appear on television, you may be applying to several shows at once. That is absolutely fine. If you find that you are being put forward to the next stage for more than one of them, think hard about which one you really want to go on. At a certain point, you will have to make a decision between the two. For *The Bachelor*, for example, the terms and conditions of the application state that you must tell the producers if you have appeared on another show and that if you are currently being considered as a contestant in a primetime reality/game show, you must withdraw your application from such competing shows on the producer's request.

Again, honesty is always the best policy. Let the production team know that you are in the running for another show. The chances are they will either put your name to one side to be considered for another programme or series or they will push hard for you to stick with their show (a good indication that they like you and want you to appear).

Appearing as an expert – be selective

If you are putting yourself forward as an expert, you should also think carefully about where you choose to appear. If you start to become 'rent-an-expert', programmes will take note and the invitations may well dry up. Nobody wants their viewers switching off because a contributor has been seen so many times before people do not bother to listen to what they say. Perhaps the only reason that multi-appearances become acceptable is if you are *the* expert on a particular subject, the person everyone has to go to because you are the only one, for example, who knows absolutely everything about a small rodent from the jungles of Madagascar.

Television programmes like to be exclusive but they also appreciate that there are only so many experts they can find and use. It is a careful balancing act. If you are going to appear on more than one show at a time, or within a short space of time, keep the production people informed.

Should you include photos with your application?

Pictures are extremely important, especially for programmes like *Queer Eye For The Straight Guy*, *The Biggest Loser*, *Coleen's Real Women*, *How To Look Good Naked* and *Open Gardens*; even *Mastermind*, *The Mole* and *Eggheads* ask for photos. It is a way for the production and casting team to fix a face to a name.

- If the application asks for photographs and you don't send any in, you will not be considered.
- As long as the picture portrays what the programme is asking for, the researchers don't care if it is taken with the latest digital technology or an old camera.
- In most cases, the production team will not return the photos so try to avoid sending your precious originals if you want them back.
- Don't send framed photos – they cannot send those back either. Having spoken to researchers and casting producers, it is extraordinary how many times they have been sent a framed picture that has obviously just been taken off the wall. Get a copy made and send that.
- If they ask for two photos and you send them ten that will not really matter. While it is always helpful for the team to see just what you are like, it does not mean that more, rather than less, will definitely get you to the next stage.
- You are not necessarily entering a beauty contest (again, it depends on the individual programme) so do not aim for glamour.
- Quite a few programmes (if they are about looks, fashion, body shape, etc.) will ask for either an underwear or swimwear shot and no make-up.
- No naked pictures, no matter how gorgeous you are.

If you really do have to send in an original photo (or any original document for that matter), make sure you write your name and address on anything that you send into a production company.

Appearing on a show – terms and conditions

The terms and conditions of appearing on a show will either appear on the website (as a link) or will be sent with the application form. You should not ignore them and read them through before sending in your form. There should not be anything controversial hidden in the small print but, by reading the details, you can make sure that:

- you are eligible for the programme
- you know what to expect.

By submitting the application form, you are saying that you accept the programme's terms and conditions.

Application forms are treated as confidential documents. Only the people working in the casting department or on the programme will have access to them.

Following up an application form or video

Established programmes get literally thousands of application forms every year. For example:

- *10 Years Younger* in the UK gets between 10,000 to 20,000 application forms
- *The Real World* has around 35,000 people apply per series
- *Shipwrecked* got over 100,000 applications
- *The Amazing Race* has over 60,000 *new* teams applying each year
- *The Biggest Loser* series four had over 100,000 people apply
- *Wheel of Fortune* has over a million people applying every year.

That is a lot of forms and videos for the researchers and casting team to sort through and remember.

You could phone up and check if your application has arrived and the production company or casting department may well make earnest efforts to see that it has but, in reality, it is very difficult for them. It is hard for the casting professionals or production office to lay their hands on your form or video immediately. It may well be sitting in the middle of a pile of several thousand.

To be honest, many of the production companies just do not have the time and would not know which pile to start checking in. So if you have any concerns that your application did not reach its destination, send it in again with a short covering note saying you were worried that the last one went missing. Don't expect an acknowledgement of receipt though. If you really want to make sure your tape or video reaches its intended destination, send it special delivery or via one of the major courier companies.

Did you know?

• The number of applicants for BBC1's *The Apprentice* went from 10,000 for series three to 20,000 for series four.
• Around 7500 people applied for the first series of *Survivor* in 2000. By series two, *Survivor Australia*, that number had leapt to 70,000.

Dealing with rejection

'If you don't hear from us at the application form stage, assume you haven't been picked for this particular series. However, we always keep the potential application forms that didn't quite make it for one reason or another. We've got forms going back three years or more. Just because you were not suitable for this series doesn't mean you won't get picked up in another.'

(Kirsty Lord, assistant producer of *10 Years Younger*)

Every programme is a balancing act: a mix of different geographical locations, a balance of male and female; young versus old and so on. This means that you should not think of giving up if your first application does not get you anywhere. Don't take the rejection to heart; there could be any number of reasons why you did not make it.

Frustratingly, at this stage, you will not know whether you did not make it further because you were just not right for the programme, or people were better than you or your application form lacked a bit of pizazz. Never mind. Think positively. That first application was a practice. Use the experience and work on making your second one even better.

'In property programmes, as with other programmes, it's mainly the circumstances that are important rather than the people themselves. If you're making a series on selling and buying houses and you've already lined up a bungalow and a villa, you don't want another bungalow or villa; you're now looking for a country cottage or a penthouse apartment. It's like casting for a drama. You have to understand that individuals need to be part of a greater whole; most programmes are made as a series rather than one offs. You don't want your programme to be full of middle-class white people from Guildford – not that there's anything wrong with them – but you need a different mix to make it interesting.'

(Mark Downie, executive producer of *Embarrassing Illnesses*; former commissioning editor, Channel 4 daytime)

Case study: quiz shows

'Every single television company does a huge amount of cold calling for contestants for a quiz show. I've phoned loads of companies, asking them to pass on the information about our show to their staff. This is better from our point of view because we tend to get new faces, a different kind of contributor from the ones who advertise on the beonscreen, StarNow type of sites. Where we look will depend on the show I'm working on; we'll tailor our search. For example, on *The Great Pretender*, which was all about bluffing, we approached firms of estate agents! The main thing people need is to be a very bubbly, big personality; someone who's comfortable having a laugh. Personality counts for a huge amount. A quiz show has got to be fun to watch. You can tell the difference when people are enjoying themselves.

For most quiz shows, you will have to do a short test. For example, on *The Great Pretender*, people were asked ten general knowledge questions. The idea is not to rule them out but to work out what level of knowledge they have. It would be no good putting someone who got three out of ten up against someone who got ten out of ten.

So, let's say you see the advert for the show and you're interested. You get an application form that asks questions that relate to the show. On *It's Not What You Know*, which needed teams of two, we asked them to tell us about their partner.

We get thousands of forms in. The ones that stand out are the ones that write more. If you're asked "Why do you want to go on the show?" don't just say "To win money and have fun." That won't get you on. Put some effort into it and be a bit imaginative. You're not filling in a CV for a job. Write how you would say it to a friend.

If their application form looks good, we give them a call and chat to them over the phone. Then, if we like what we hear, we'll ask them to an audition. When someone answers the phone, you can tell straightaway by their response whether they're going to be good or not. If they're bubbly and excited that they've got a call from you, then you get a feel for their character. If all you get are one-word answers and they sound a bit flat, you don't really want to see them.

We have to go all over the UK to meet people. We need more people per programme than are actually used. So we do have stand-ins. For *It's Not What You Know*, we had a run of 30 shows and for that we needed between 50 to 60 couples. We saw 60 couples at each audition location.

On the phone and at the auditions, you will get asked the same sort of questions that were on the application form – particularly "What would you spend the money on?" We're not going to hold you to your answer or check up on you if you do win the money. I would suggest that you try and think of something a bit different, something more interesting than "I'm going to pay off the mortgage". When it comes to the show, Chris Tarrant will ask contestants this. If your answer is amusing, funny, or quirky, it's better for the show. It helps the programme makers to write their script.

Each audition is different depending on the show. You play a version of the game, especially if it's a new one because you need to understand it. You usually only get one audition and that's the only time you play the game before being filmed on the show. For *It's Not What You Know*, we had six couples at a time; we got them to do a question each, then we played the game as a group so we could see how they interacted with each other. It does count for a lot to be jokey with the group – try and have a laugh and be excited about being auditioned.

We film auditions. People will be asked to do a piece to camera; explain how they know each other, tell funny stories – very generic stuff. You will always be asked these kind of questions, so bear that in mind. We've had some really great stories and we use them to write the script for the show.

Be prepared to sell yourself. We are looking to put you on television in front of the nation. We need to find people who can laugh, have a joke and not be serious. Don't be nervous because that can affect you. Remember, it's not really a big deal; you're doing it for fun. In the grand scheme of things, it's not that important; you're not going to look back on your death bed and think, "I wish I'd got on that show". If you don't get on one, you can always try another show.

If you are not asked on, it's not because you were rubbish. When we are doing 30 shows, we want lots of different permutations of couples (mother and daughter; father and son, and so on). We can't pick all father and son teams from the north, for example. It's luck whether you come up against someone who is your same age and type. If you don't get on, it's not necessarily a reflection of your personality.

On *It's Not What You Know*, we worked with a series producer. We showed him the tapes of the auditions when we got back to the office. We noted down the ones we thought were good. Once we'd seen everyone, we sat down together, went through our notes, discussed everything and watched the tapes again. For every series, we end up with hundreds of casting sheets before we narrow it down.

If you haven't heard from us, then you've been unsuccessful. It's not that we can't be bothered to phone people up to let them know. There were only two researchers, myself and another, doing the casting for *It's Not What You Know* and that's not unusual. We can't phone everyone up because we will have seen so many. There's only ten weeks to set up the show, advertise and find people, do auditions and then film all the shows; time is very tight.

We write biogs [short biographies] on each contestant which is then given to the scriptwriter, before being given to the presenter. You may get several phone calls before filming from researchers checking up on information for your biog. We brief our contestants fully beforehand so they know what to expect. We will pay your expenses and you will get put up in a hotel if you live a long way away. Bear in mind your availability; we expect people to take a day off work. If you want to be on the show, you have to appreciate you might have to work round our timetable and not the other way around.

We film three programmes a day which is fairly standard practice. This is because studios are expensive so you want to get the most out of your day's filming. We did 30 shows in two weeks, working weekdays and weekends. Filming an hour-long show can sometimes take up to four hours to record; we do pick-up shots; we make you do things again and again. These are long days. Even if you are in the last show to be filmed that day, you will be asked to turn up early because the briefing is given to all three shows' contestants. The plus side of that is you get to see two shows being filmed beforehand. We do try and make your day as fun as possible. Chris Tarrant is brilliant with the contestants; he treats them like his mates and is really friendly. We want our people to feel like celebrities for the day so we make sure you do have a wonderful day.'

(Joanne Price, quiz show researcher)

04

auditions –
the screening
process

In this chapter you will learn:
- how to pass the telephone
  interview test
- how to prepare for a filmed
  audition or open casting call
- the importance of
  presentation
- how to behave.

*Television enables you to be entertained in your home by
people you wouldn't have at home.*

(David Frost, broadcaster)

Making an impression

'When we are looking for potential contributors, we want people
who are engaging on screen and that have a sense of life about
them. On the phone, that can be tricky to gauge so we are looking
for clues that suggest you'd be good on-screen. But don't try to
pretend to be someone you're not; we can spot that too!'

(Martha Housden, development producer)

This is a massively important next step – when someone from
the production team actually gets to speak to you and, very
often, film you. This is where you need to show your character,
that you can tell your story, that you are able to speak about
yourself, what you are feeling (without going into too much
detail – this is a television programme, not a session with a
psychiatrist) and what you want to get out of the experience.

The process will depend on where you are applying. In the UK,
after the application form stage, there are likely to be two more
stages before you get the thumbs up: a telephone interview and
then a filmed interview or audition. It will depend on the
individual programme whether they do one or both stages.
Daily shows, for example, are usually done on the phone;
makeover programmes will want to talk to you, then see you,
and talent shows skip the telephone interview and go straight to
the audition stage for every potential participant.

In the US, video applications are common, with written
application forms running a close second. However, mass open
auditions (or casting calls) for some reality programmes are
much more widespread in the US than in the UK. Casting teams
will set up open castings in major cities around the US and invite
people to 'just turn up'. They give you very little time to make
an impression but at least you get the opportunity to perform on
the casting team's cameras and show off your personality. Do be
aware, though, that not all reality TV programmes have the
budget to travel around the country so living on or near the
West and East coasts, close to Los Angeles and New York, does
have its advantages.

The phone interview

'Researchers will do everything in their power to help your application process. People should realise that we're doing a job but we want the best for our potential contributors. Just be confident; be warm and giving of yourself. Tell us your story. Who are you? What's your family like? Make yourself sound interesting. You need to paint a picture of who you are to the person at the other end of the line.'

(Chloe Nisbet, researcher on *10 Years Younger*)

Production companies will try and talk to as many people as they can. The written word only gives the team basic information. What the television people need to know is whether you can *tell* your story as well as write it. The telephone interview is the verbal equivalent of the application form. For television, being able to talk is much more important than writing.

The people doing these phone interviews are mainly researchers (in the UK) and casting professionals (in the US). As with the application form stage, they have the power to give the thumbs up (or down) on someone. Series producers and show runners rely on them to do the legwork and sort through the long list of potential contributors.

Just because it is done on the phone with a friendly, chatty person, it is still an interview. The researcher or casting professional want it to be a casual conversation, rather than something more formal, because they want to find out what your personality is really like. But remember that they will be listening very hard to the answers you give and how you talk. Don't get too relaxed; this is your moment to sell yourself.

And you can sell yourself more successfully if you *are* yourself. There is no need to put on airs, or try and speak 'properly' or act as if you are applying for a real job. Just as it does not really matter if you do not get every sentence grammatically spot-on and every word spelt correctly on your application form, it is not important here if you drop your aitches or have a broad accent. What you do need is to be able to tell your story and give a sense of your personality.

If you are asked to compare yourself with someone who appeared on a previous show ... then DON'T! This is a trick question. You are not a carbon copy of someone; you are a unique individual and that is what the programme is looking for. You may feel that you could be the twin of Tiffany Pollard or Connie Fisher but don't let on to the interviewer that you feel like that. Tell them that you cannot really pigeonhole yourself; you want to bring unique qualities to their programme, not a repeat performance.

What should you expect from a phone interview?

You will spend half an hour to an hour talking with a researcher, casting professional, assistant producer, perhaps even a producer. They will check you and your story out, putting the meat on the bones of information that you gave in your application form.

You should get used to being asked similar questions again and again. The questions that you answered on your application form will come up in the telephone interview and again, if you get through to the filmed interview. The production team are not necessarily trying to catch you out; it is just that programmes have to take great care with people and their stories, because:

- programmes like *The Steve Wilkos Show* or *Jeremy Kyle*, for example, talk to some very vulnerable people (with drink or drug problems, eating disorders or traumatic relationships)
- makeover programmes will see people hit emotional highs and lows
- physical programmes (*American Gladiator*, *Unbreakable*, *The Alaska Experiment*) put contributors through challenging and tough tasks.

Are you physically and mentally able to cope with the rigours of making a programme? The production team has a duty of care for the people they are dealing with. They want to be sure that what you are telling them are the facts and, at the same time, make sure that you are confident with your story and happy with how you are telling it.

Despite the same questions coming up yet again, make sure you are interested in what you are saying. It does not matter if you feel you are repeating yourself again. If you sound bored with what you are saying, you will come over as a bit flat and dull and that is a big turn-off for the person at the other end of the line. You need to put meaning into what you are saying. If you are describing a sad event, sound sad; if it was an amazing experience, sound upbeat and energized. In order to sound natural, you almost have to caricature your natural self. Put a bit more energy and feeling into it and you will make an impact on the person who is interviewing you.

> Change the pitch of your voice as you are speaking. It makes your voice more musical, doesn't rely on you having to turn up the volume to grab someone's attention and makes what you are saying more interesting to the listener.

These conversations can work to your advantage. It is also *your* time to ask as many questions of the production team as you want. You can find out what people are looking for, what is involved in the programme and whether you really want to be part of it. By having this staggered interview process, you can make sure of what you are getting into.

> 'We're looking for a spark but that doesn't mean you have to be wildly OTT. For a makeover programme, we might ask questions like "How old do you think you look and why?" If all you can say to that is "Crow's feet" and, despite gentle probing, you can't say anything more, then that's not good. We need you to tell us your story, not give one-word answers.'
>
> (Kirsty Lord, assistant producer of *10 Years Younger*)

What to do if you can't take the phone call

As with any phone call, it is sometimes just not convenient to take it; you might be in the middle of something (the kids are screaming for their supper, you're in the shower or you're driving in the car) or so taken aback by being phoned up by the TV company that you feel a bit tongue-tied.

You will *not* blow your chance with the programme makers if you ask them to call at a more convenient time; they will call you back later on. If they are phoning you up at this stage, they are already interested in you. They want to see if you have got what they are looking for. Just be polite and explain that it is not really convenient right now and give them a time when you are able to talk. Look on the positive side: it gives you a breathing space to prepare yourself for the interview rather than having to cope with it out of the blue.

- Gather your thoughts (and the copy of your application form, if you can, to remind yourself what you wrote).
- Remind yourself of what your character is and what your story is all about.
- Then get yourself mentally prepared to have a 'friendly chat' that will show off your unique personality and qualities – enough to make the interviewer want to meet you in person.

'With telephone interviews, if the person I'm talking to interests me then I want to meet them. If you find you get on with them, their personality comes to life. You make a connection and build a rapport with each other.'

(Madonna Benjamin, executive producer of *Born Too Soon*, *The Madness Of Modern Families* and *Who Gets Custody Of The Dog?*)

Even though the person at the other end of the line cannot see you, sit up (or stand if it makes you feel more dynamic and in control). Slouching in your chair and muttering will not make you sound bubbly and interesting. It is a mixture of being alert and on the ball but relaxed at the same time. If you can manage to do that, it will come over in your voice.

'It's not a question of selling yourself but being yourself. I don't want the hard sell. It's like meeting someone in the pub and thinking "Oh, I like you; you're fun." Something that helps is good energy. You'd be amazed at how many people I've seen who want to be on television but look bored and mumble. We want life, energy.'

(Mark Downie, executive producer of *Embarrassing Illnesses*; former commissioning editor, Channel 4 daytime)

Afterwards

After telephone interviews, the production/casting team will sit down together and have a conversation in the office about all the people they have spoken to and who stood out for them. They will then decide who is worth seeing face to face for the next stage of auditions. If the programme is UK-based, it depends on the particular programme whether you are asked to go to the production offices or they travel to you.

Some production companies, both in the UK and the US, favour open casting calls and will go to five or six locations around the country, auditioning in different cities (such as *Wheel Of Fortune, Big Brother, It's Not What You Know*). Do remember that at this stage if you are asked to go to the production company's office (in the UK) or open casting calls (UK or US), it is unlikely that you will get paid travelling expenses for this.

It is important not to let yourself get caught out. The way programmes will pick people change from year to year and series to series. For example:

- *The X Factor* dropped the age limit to 14 and changed the way they ran their bootcamps (from splitting them up between different locations for two days, to gathering everyone together in one location for four days)
- *American Idol* changed the upper age limit in the fourth season, to 28 years old
- *10 Years Younger* used to have one interview, held at the production company's offices; that was changed to a two-stage process – people were filmed at the production team's offices which, if the individual was felt to be a good prospect, was followed up with a home visit.

If you have been interested in getting on a programme for some time and have researched what that particular programme's screening process was, don't be surprised if, when you get there, it has changed. Prepare yourself to expect change; do not let a different procedure that you were not expecting put you off or unnerve you. Be flexible and adapt to the situation as quickly as you can; this will stand you in good stead during filming as well.

Researchers will interview loads of people on the phone; for *Embarrassing Illnesses,* the researchers talk to around 1000 people, whittled down from the application forms. They then bring around 100 to 200 to the offices for a short filmed interview. After that, they go to see about 30 to 40 people in their own homes. For *Survivor* a total of 800 make it to the semi-finals which are held in cities around the US. Approximately 48 are invited to the final pick in Los Angeles, from where around 16 men and women make it onto the programme.

'It's a question of extremes, isn't it? If someone is naturally extremely boring or extremely OTT then, as programme makers, we can make something out of this and turn it into a story. You need to be 10 to 20 per cent above or below the norm. If you're a joker, you need to be 10 per cent more than the average joker. I suppose that's called charisma. That doesn't mean we want people to reach pantomime levels or become cartoon characters but to stand out just enough to shine on TV. Reality, in the truest, most ordinary sense, doesn't make good television.'

(Neil Edwards, executive producer of *How To Have Sex After Marriage*, *Open Gardens*, *The Estate We're In*, *The Hotel Inspector* and *Life Begins Again*)

Auditions – be safe

'For us, when it comes to casting, it's location, location, location. Most production companies work out of LA or New York so when they cast shows, they are essentially looking in these areas because travel is so prohibitively expensive. So, if you're in or near those cities or a few hours travel away, you have a better chance of getting on the show.

A handful of shows have the budget to travel; they'll do open castings around the country and fly their finalists to LA or New York (like *Big Brother* or *Deal Or No Deal*) but that's not the case for all programmes. As frustrating as it is, we are limited by the area we work in. Our talent pools are dictated by geography so we cast our nets close to where we are based. Some people do offer to travel to us which is great. But, with our show, we want to focus on the subject's lifestyle, their family, their friends, where they live and work so we need to go to them, not the other way round.'

(Riaz Patel, executive producer of *How To Look Good Naked*, *Ultimates*, *Why Can't I Be You?* and *Into Character*)

There should be no problems when you turn up at an audition. Ninety nine times out of a hundred, they will be for reputable programmes, run by established production companies and casting departments. However, it is always sensible to be careful and make sure that you do not put yourself in a vulnerable position.

- Get all the information on the audition (where you have to go, who you will be seeing, a contact phone number) from the company before you go.
- Check out the company on the internet before the audition; a reputable company should have a website and very probably details of the open auditions.
- If you are travelling to the audition on your own, tell a friend or relative where you are going and leave details of the address. Give them a time when you expect to be finished.
- Reputable auditions are held in public places (football stadiums, shopping malls and convention centres are popular venues). Don't attend auditions that are held at residential addresses.
- If you are told that you will have to pay to attend the audition, then decline it. You should never have to do this.
- Don't feel you have to be pressurized into doing anything you are not comfortable with.
- If you are asked to sign anything (a contract, release form), take the time to read it through. If you are unsure of anything, ask for an explanation.

Case study: *Big Brother* auditions

The auditions will roughly go along the following stages but don't be surprised if this changes. Most production companies will always tweak and refine their selection process and *Big Brother* is no different. The process also differs slightly from country to country. Remember that the production company and casting department is also looking for different individuals and an interesting mix of people for each series. Don't try and 'act' like a housemate; just be yourself. It could be enough to get you through.

- If you are applying for the US series, you will first need to fill in a 12-page application form (answering questions such as: What are you afraid of and why? Have you ever been to a nude beach? What would you do if BB made you famous?) and provide a two-minute audition video (saying why you would make the ultimate housemate). You will also indicate which one of the semi-final locations you would be willing to travel to (at your own expense).
- In the UK, you can submit an application form and short (one to two minutes) video application or you can turn up to the open auditions. There, after waiting in line and then doing a bit

of a warm-up, you will be put into groups of around eight to ten where you will be asked to do things such as arrange your group in order of attractiveness (ugly one end, good-looking the other) or you will be split into pairs with someone you don't know and you have to find out about each other then tell your group what you've found out.

- Those who then get a stamp on their hand are through to the next stage where a photo will be taken and you will have a quick filmed interview with a couple of producers who will ask you about yourself.

- You are then given a very comprehensive application form to fill in (40-plus pages) that asks very personal questions, for example: When did you lose your virginity? Would you pose naked?

- Those who are successful at the open auditions will be asked back a day or so later. Then it's into a mock-up of the diary room where you are again interviewed.

- You won't hear anything for a few weeks; if you've got through this stage, you will be asked to attend another audition, along with a group of other potential housemates.

The filmed interview

'Whether applying for *How To Look Good Naked* or *Grand Designs*, there are certain generic things being looked for. Passion, a spark, is paramount. A good contributor is not a wannabe.'

(Andrew Anderson, executive producer of *Property Ladder*, *House Doctor*, *Families Behaving Badly* and *10 Years Younger*)

Broadcasters seem more cautious about commissioning programmes and people off paper. They actually want to see people on tape. So pre-casting is much more prevalent now. If, after phoning a contestant hotline or sending in an application form/video, you are told that they want to see you for an audition interview, then congratulate yourself; you have got through quite a few selection processes already.

In the US, you may get called to one of several major cities around the country for this semi-final stage. In the UK, a production team may well ask people to come to their production offices. They want to get them in front of the camera to see if they have a story and that special character that makes them stand out from everyone else. If it is for a makeover programme, they would like to see someone, in the words of a member of one makeover team, who is a bit 'ropey'; perhaps another way of putting it is that they don't want them looking their best. Whereas if you are going for a screen test as an expert you certainly do need to look professional and well turned out.

> Think back to the character you are going to present yourself as; dress, talk and behave in character at all times.

Making an impression and losing those nerves

'If you've got it, flaunt it.' But what is 'it'? People who have this elusive quality stand out in a crowd. And that is handy if you are going through the audition process for a television programme.

'It' seems to translate as a special kind of energy or charisma. From the minute you get up in the morning to when you walk into the audition room, you need to tap into that energy. An actor has to be ready to perform at the drop of a hat. Like an actor, you have to be ready to switch on and perform when the interviewer or judges give you the go-ahead.

- As you travel to the audition, don't lose yourself in a book or a magazine. Be aware of what is going on; feed off the energy that surrounds you.
- Imagine you are 'on show' from the moment you walk into the production company's building or wherever the auditions are being held. You aren't necessarily being judged then (although you don't know that) but you should get into character right from the start. Be friendly and polite to members of staff and engage with your fellow auditionees.
- If members of the production team are coming to you, don't lose yourself in household chores. Concentrate on your surroundings; build up a sense of that energy while you wait for them to arrive.
- Run through the interview scenario in your head beforehand. Imagine walking in and seeing a man or woman (or a whole

panel of judges). Now imagine them being friendly, then imagine them being really formal. Then picture yourself walking in, looking them in the eye, shaking hands, smiling. It really helps to try and imagine the different kinds of people and atmospheres you could encounter.

- When you are called in for the interview, walk in with confidence and introduce yourself.
- See the case study tips on page 113 for more techniques to prepare yourself for auditions and interviews.

You may well get asked the same question several times – don't be fazed by this. It means that the interviewer thinks you have got something worth recording and just wants to show you in your best light by coaching and coaxing the answer out of you. Take the hint and let them lead you into giving the answer they are after. That does not mean lie, of course. They are not saying they don't like your answer or want you to change it. What they want is for you to say it more succinctly, or by telling a particular anecdote, or with more enthusiasm. Take their direction; they know what they are talking about.

Being articulate and lively is a good thing but that is not enough to get you through. You also have to be aware that you may well get asked some tough questions at this stage; the production team will want to know everything about you. They don't want surprises once they have started this process. This is partly because some production companies have been stung in the past by serial contributors and they want to make sure you are not that kind of person. Also, it helps prepare you for the real experience, when the cameras are turned on and recording you for real.

'We interview people at the offices on camera. We control it because we have a list of questions that we want answering – usually the same as the application form. You must expect the same questions again and again! This is the way the process builds. It's more of a conversation than an interview – just be yourself because that's what we're looking for. I've had times when the person in front of the camera will say, "Oh, turn the camera off. Now, how do you want me to answer that?" That's not what we want. If we have to ask the same question six times or more, we will. If we see something in you that we want to bring out, we will try our hardest to get you to give us that. This 'interview' can last 15 minutes or three hours. The length of the interview doesn't indicate whether you're going on to the next stage or not. A short interview can mean you may go on or you may stop there – just the same as a long interview. Don't read anything into it.'

(Kirsty Lord, assistant producer of *10 Years Younger*)

The table interview

Bunim-Murray, producers of *The Real World*, are responsible for developing a style of auditioning that has since been adopted by many other reality TV programmes (such as *The Swan* and *The Apprentice*). The 'table' interview method is a good way of seeing how people interact with each other and what their personality is like.

You will be seated around a table with eight or nine other hopefuls plus a casting director who will ask the group a few questions to get a conversation going. This will not be a genteel, polite chat. These questions are designed to get strong answers out of people in order to find out who is the most self-confident, who is the funniest, who is the peace maker and so on. The whole process will only take ten minutes so you need to make your impact and show your character in a fairly short space of time.

- You will probably find yourself sitting round the table with the people you have been standing in line with. If you have been chatting to them and paying attention, you will already have an idea of who the strong characters are. These are the ones to watch. Make sure you do not get over-shadowed by them during the table interview.
- Don't try to be someone you are not; remember your 'character' – that is who you should be.
- If you are in a room full of people to be interviewed, do not assume that they are all potential candidates like you. One or two may be from the production/casting team. Equally, if you have to sit round a table, don't think that the person at the head of the table observing everyone is in charge; it may be just another hopeful.

If you have travelled to be interviewed, you may be filmed on your own or in groups. Whether you are being filmed in a group or on your own, take a note of your surroundings. You can be filmed in a variety of different rooms; you will not necessarily be filmed in a studio location. If it is an ordinary room, make sure you sit slightly at an angle to the camera (you will look better on camera this way) and turn yourself away from direct sunlight or windows. This also applies if you are being interviewed at home; don't let the familiarity of your surroundings lull you into being too relaxed.

'If someone really wants to do [the programme], I don't want them. If anyone is too keen then they are probably not right. A lot of *Wife Swap* people were not chosen because of this. Very 'ordinary' is not a good thing; people have to stand out. Yes, we want character, eccentricity – but they must be honest. You don't have to be too nice. If you're chaotic, say you are. Fix yourself in a producer's head. Entertain. Show a sense of humour. That gets you to the next stage.'

(Emma Glasser, development producer)

Being interviewed

Zoe Case, a researcher on *10 Years Younger* and *Embarrassing Illnesses* explains that when being interviewed, it's important to consider your reply and answer in full sentences: 'It's a strange TV way of speaking. It has to make sense if the questions were taken out. For example, if you were asked where you lived, don't just say "Birmingham". You should say, in reply to "Where do you come from?" "I come from Birmingham." This is because it makes the editing process so much easier. And someone who can speak effectively like this is an attractive prospect as a contributor.' Here are Zoe's tips for what makes a successful interview.

- Feel free to cry, laugh or make a joke. It makes you appear human and often these are the best bits.
- If asked to say something again but shorter/longer/quicker/slower, don't be offended. This means that we like what you are saying but want you to say it so it sounds better.
- Don't look down the lens of the camera – you're not a presenter.

- If you find it hard to look at the person who is asking you questions, focus on a spot on their shoulder or behind their head.
- This is your time. Feel free to say something again if you think you haven't said it right. If, at the end of the interview, you think there's something that you really want to say, then say it.
- This process isn't live so you can say things as many times as you want.
- Don't do overlapping – leave a beat after the interviewer has asked you a question. This helps for editing and, if you're making life easier for the production team, you tend to shine more.
- We have two minutes, if we're lucky, to sell our contributor to our producers so we want them to appear at their best.
- Out of a 20- to 40-minute chat, only two minutes will be seen – at most. Use your researcher; trust them because they want you to come across and shine.
- You should be told all of this by your researcher but it can sometimes be forgotten if you're number eight or nine in a long list of interviews. Just be prepared.

The quiz and game show interview

Quiz and game shows have remained a constant favourite in the TV schedules for years. Not all quiz shows are about answering general knowledge questions; some involve decision-making (such as *Deal Or No Deal* or *Golden Balls*), bluffing (*The Mole* and *The Great Pretender*) or dating (*Dirty Cows* and *The Bachelor*). So you do not have to be brilliant at lots of subjects to take part.

The first time you will get to actually play the game is during the filmed auditions; the second time will be for real, in a TV studio. So if you are going for a new show, pay attention to the rules! If you are auditioning for a show that is already on the air, play along with the show at home so that you are familiar with the rules and how the show works and can match or, at the very least, come close to the performance of the contestants.

> If you are part of a team, make sure there is a combination of males and females because that will improve your chances of getting onto the show. Programme makers like to have a mix.

Have your anecdotes to hand and be ready to use them. You should already have been asked at the application form stage for anecdotes (a 'funny' story about your team-mates, what you would do with the prize money should you win or a dating disaster). The casting team will ask you to tell your story; you need to show that you are articulate and able to get that story over without rambling on or losing the thread of your story.

'Funny' anecdotes are one thing; trying to make yourself stand out as a comedian can be tricky. Humour is subjective and this is not the time to try and crack a joke at the presenter's expense.

At auditions for *The Weakest Link*, you get to play the game and then you have a filmed interview where the researcher is likely to ask you about your tactics for the show and why you voted the way you did in the practice game. This is a great opportunity to make yourself stand out from the others. Think about what makes the show entertaining. People being nice and reasonable to each other or being hard-nosed, tactical and firing off witty one-liners?

Be careful about revealing too much at this stage of the game. Now may not be the time to show off your superior general knowledge; perhaps it might be better to get a few questions wrong. Production teams like their quizzes to be exciting contests and what is exciting about someone getting all the answers right? Where is the competition? The nail biting head-to-head at the end of the show? Production companies also like to match up contestants of similar knowledge. Unless you can guarantee that there will be other contestants at the same level as you, you could aim to get a few wrong so you have the edge when it comes to the show.

Quiz shows are all about entertainment so you need to show that you are bubbly, bright, vivacious and full of energy ... even if you don't get all the questions right. It is not about winning at this stage. It is all about showing your personality, your enthusiasm and your ability to play the game.

Did you know?

- In 1992, Vanna White, the hostess on *Wheel Of Fortune*, became the world's most frequent clapper (according to the Guinness Book of World Records). She applauds contestants around 28,080 times a season which works out at an average of 720 times each show.

- 200,700 questions were written for BBC1's 2007 show *The People's Quiz* although only about a quarter were released to the public.

The makeover show interview

These programmes are about inspiration for others so, although you have probably had some difficult times, this is not an opportunity to go on about how depressing life is. You have to genuinely want to *change* your life (or house, or garden, boyfriend or dog).

Be honest about your situation: if you have lived in sweatpants for the last five years, don't dress up as if you are going for a job interview. They want to see the real you. The same goes for the house or the garden – don't tidy up, let them see it as it is.

Producers will also want to see the emotional ups and downs of this change, so there will be some tough questioning. If you are putting yourself forward, you must be prepared for a thorough grilling.

The researcher or other member of the casting team will do the interview at this point but they are not the ones who will be able to tell you whether you are a 'Yes' or a 'No', so it is not worth questioning them to find out. People who cast for reality TV shows constantly go out to interview people, spend hours with them, positive that they were bound to be used because they were great, only to get back to the production team and find out they are a 'No' because someone else was even 'better' ('better' being whatever the team are looking for at that time).

'I will speak to potential contributors further down the line, after the application form and recce stage; I'll phone them up. If I sense the slightest nerves, I cross them off my list. That's probably harsh but you have to be ruthless; you don't want to end up with egg on your face. If I have the tiniest bit of doubt, I don't use them. I've seen it happen before. You get to a live show and your contributor freezes – it can be a huge problem. Therefore you have to be brutal. If people stutter and stumble, that's not a problem; we don't expect polished speaking. What I'm looking for is confidence, naturalness and, hopefully, something unique. With experience, you can pretty much tell instantly if someone will be OK: if you engage each other in conversation; if you can sense their honesty and if you sense that they're prepared to commit to the process for you. If they're not going to commit fully, you could have big problems later on in the production. That's why it's important for us to be honest and upfront right from the start with our contributors. They need to trust us. But if they start crying or explode with anger in front of the camera, then they should not expect us to stop; in almost all cases we will continue rolling because these are the moments in a television programme that we're looking for. They're not the be all and end all of a show, but it's these moments that usually provide the drama and emotion that keep the viewer engaged.

If you're not prepared to let your guard down a bit, expose your emotions or even look foolish or silly at some point during the filming, then pick your television programmes carefully. Most of us aren't out to stitch you up but a good story, by its very nature, has its highs and lows. And those highs and lows are your highs and lows. So be prepared to be open about your failures as well as your successes. We all like a happy ending, but a happy beginning and middle too makes for a pretty flat story.'

(Neil Edwards, executive producer of *How To Have Sex After Marriage*, *Open Gardens*, *The Estate We're In*, *The Hotel Inspector* and *Life Begins Again*)

The talent show audition

'The joy of *Big Brother* is people turning up off the street who you'd never think would have applied or even want to apply. The *Big Brother* team at Endemol do all the hard legwork, running open auditions around the country and seeing thousands of people. Then they have what they call a 'boardroom day' where they sit down with a tape of around 80 to 90 filmed interviews; they spend two days watching the tapes while they whittle the group down. At Channel 4, we get to see these final interviews when the list reaches 30 people. The first group of housemates will be chosen from this final group. But we need a pool of people to choose from. [For example, *Big Brother* series seven used a total of 24 housemates in the end; the US production team aim to get a pool of around 40 finalists.]

Everybody who goes through the audition process is being observed by members of the production team, from the first warm-up to the final interviews. You're watched pretty much all the time. Certain people come on and think that they can 'act' a housemate ("I'll be the camp one/the flirty one/the bossy one"). We need to instill in people that it's the way they are that interests us, not what they're pretending to be. My advice is to be yourself. Audiences are more sophisticated, they can spot a fraud a mile off.'

(David Williams, commissioning editor, Channel 4)

Shows like *Big Brother, How Do You Solve A Problem Like Maria?, Grease Is The Word, American Idol* and *Britain's/America's Got Talent* are incredibly popular – both for the viewers and the people who want to take part in them. *The X Factor*, which began in 2004 had a mere 50,000 people attend the various auditions held around the country for the first series; by series three, that number had grown to 100,000. Around 10,000 (or more) people will turn up at just one audition venue for the chance to be on *American Idol*.

With thousands queuing round the block, the odds against getting through are enormous. The same rules of getting a diverse and balanced mix of performers in a programme applies here as well. Even if the ten best singers of the lot were all from Devon, 19 years old, female and blonde, it would be unlikely that the programme makers would cast all of them; they would also give the nod to people of different ages, backgrounds, sex, hair colour, and, let's be honest, talent.

Having said all that, these production teams need performers to make the programme in the first place; *someone* has to get on the television and win and it might very well be you. The entertainment industry is a tough nut to crack (as are these auditions). Programmes like this can be the most amazing launch pad for really talented people. So stack the odds a bit more in your favour by being prepared for the selection process.

In nearly every case, you will only have a minute or two, if you are lucky, to sell yourself to the first set of judges, who will probably be members of the production company or the casting department; the 'real' judges appear later on in the process. That is just a few minutes of intensity after standing around in a queue for several hours. That means you should practise what you are going to say. Practise in front of the mirror, practise in front of friends and family. Listen to what they say and take on board any criticisms or advice. You don't want to sound unprepared. Believe in yourself – this is your chance to pitch *you*, the singer/actor/dancer or whatever the talent you are up for. You cannot allow yourself to get sidetracked with small, fussy details or too many anecdotes.

- If there are application forms to go with your audition, you will probably be able to download them from the internet. Do this before you get to the audition; you need to take time and effort to fill them in properly (see Chapter 03), not whilst you are shuffling forward in a queue, balancing the papers on your friend's back and trying to get the pen to work.
- You will most likely have to wait a long time in a queue; this means you may be outside for a while, so dress appropriately.
- Let your clothes speak for you and say something about you. Dress comfortably. If you feel comfortable, you will perform better (although comfortable does not necessarily mean sweat pants and flip-flops).
- You will not get fed while you wait; there may be a sandwich bar nearby or, at the very least, a soft drinks machine. You need energy to perform so take along a drink and something like a banana which is easy to digest and will give you an energy boost when you need it.
- Even in the queue, you can make yourself stand out. You never know if a member of the production/casting team is around, watching how people behave. You may be auditioned in groups in which case you want to have built up a rapport and an energy with people around you – it can help.
- Be prepared: you may have three minutes or you may only have a minute. You will be told how long you have but you will not be given loads of time; if you run over, expect to get cut off in the middle of your song, dance or monologue.
- Practise what you are going to say (in your head if necessary) and do this while you wait. There are no second chances at this stage. Time limits are strictly adhered to.
- Arrive early. Even though the casting team will aim to see everybody who turns up, get there when they are feeling fresh and not after they have seen several hundred no-hopers and are beginning to lose the will to live.
- You do not have to wear a silly outfit to make yourself stand out; a chicken suit or dressing in the latest outrageous fashion will not necessarily get you onto the next stage. What you say and do is meant to be the most important thing at this point. Wearing a bikini and Wellington boots can make you stand out … for all the wrong reasons, if that is not a true representation of your personality.

- Equally, if the bikini-wellie boots look is your everyday outfit of choice, then that is fine; wear what you're comfortable in.
- Put simply, your image should reflect your personality.
- Be honest; represent yourself; don't try to act like someone else.

When you walk through the door

- Have your story ready – who you are and why you deserve to go through. You want to convince the judges of your passion for this. 'I've wanted this all my life' (even if they're barely out of kindergarten) seems to be the popular phrase for so many hopefuls. *Everyone* says this at auditions so how many times do you think the judges have heard it? Be different and convey your passion differently.
- Smile at the judges and production team – a smile helps you relax. It is also polite and connects with the people who are about to judge you.
- Take a few deep breaths and keep calm. Don't be intimidated by the judging panel. If it helps, imagine them naked ...
- Remember to listen to the judge or interviewer. You may be so keyed up to say what you want that you forget to listen. Whilst the other person is speaking, be attentive to what they are saying and take the opportunity to get breathing properly again.
- Show the judges your personality – not attitude.
- Try to be as close to your normal self as possible.

Television is show business so you need to be able to perform. It does not have to be over the top and dramatic but must be entertaining.

Simon Cowell has been quoted as saying that 99 per cent of the people he sees at the auditions are rubbish or weirdos, but at least the weirdos are entertaining rather than being nonentities. If you are honest about your 'talent' and know in your heart that you cannot really sing, act or perform, there is nevertheless the chance that you could make it to the filmed audition programmes – as one of the worst. But be warned; you will be told that you did a great performance by the production team. Singers and performers who appear to genuinely believe they have a chance – but sound like a cat being skinned – make great television.

Singing competitions

- Don't agonize too much about what song. Just choose one that will show off your voice – that is what the judges want to hear. They are not there to approve your choice of music.
- If you are asked to have two songs ready, choose two contrasting songs that will show off your vocal range.
- Rehearse your song beforehand; the judges can tell if you haven't prepared. If you show that you have got a work ethic, it is a plus point with the judges. After all, the winner will either get a record deal or star in a West End or Broadway show or something similar and they do not want the kind of person who just can't be bothered.
- If there is a song that really means something to you, sing that. Singing from your heart, your soul, can work wonders for your performance.
- Try and avoid the popular songs, the ones that everybody else will go for. The judges will have heard them many, many times before; you don't want to encourage the judges to switch off.
- You may not get to choose a song but will be given a set piece when you arrive; take every minute to run through it, get it set in your head and work out how you are going to perform it.
- You will probably be able to sing a verse and a chorus. There will be no music or musicians to accompany you so get used to singing on your own.
- Don't take backing tracks or sheet music with you.
- Sing as *you*. You are not Whitney Houston, you are not Mick Jagger … we have already got them and they perform better than you could ever do even when you are mimicking them. What the judges are looking for is something new.
- If you are singing for the chance to take part in a musical, remember to act through your song as well as sing it.
- Judge the space in which you are singing. If the judges are six feet away from you, don't pitch your voice as if they were sitting at the back of the hall.
- If you make a mistake, don't apologize or flounder. Just stop, pause, and then start again. If you can show that you can recover from a mistake with professionalism, you'll get a tick in the box next to your name.

The importance of music

If you have a song or piece of music that you know always makes you feel happy or uplifted, put it on your iPod or MP3 player and listen to it on the way to the audition. If you can arrive full of vitality and in a good mood, you have won half the battle. If you don't have a piece of feel-good music, FIND one! Everyone should have one. This is so much a question of personal taste and emotional response but music lovers have owned up to:

- Brown-Eyed Girl *Van Morrison*
- String Quintet *Schubert*
- You Raise Me Up *Westlife*
- Eye of the Tiger *Survivor*
- The Four Seasons *Vivaldi*
- Daydream Believer *The Monkees*
- Angels *Robbie Williams*
- Don't Stop Me *Now Queen*
- 2nd Piano Concerto *Rachmaninov*
- Brideshead Revisited *theme tune*
- Chariots of Fire *Vangelis*

Choose something that does it for you. Everybody's different!

Case study: getting through auditions and interviews

'When preparing for an interview or audition, draw up the questions you would ask if you were running the interview. For example:

- What are the best three things about you?
- What are the worst three things about you?
- If you got onto this programme, how would it change your life?
- What's the funniest/strangest/saddest thing that has ever happened to you?
- Tell me about your family/best friend/team member/s
- What does money mean to you?
- If you could go anywhere for a year, where would you go?

Your answers should be honest and have the ring of truth about them. And always, always be prepared for "Why do you want to come on this show?" The answer to this question, which is often the hardest to answer, should have some really personal element to it, a memory or a moment when you realised something about yourself which going on the show would achieve.

For example, if it's a quiz show with cash prizes, you could answer something along the lines of: "Like everyone, I sit at home and answer all the questions every week and watch people carry home £5000 (or $250,000 or £/$1 million) and I just feel I've got to give myself the chance because it's the only way I can treat my kids to a holiday/give my wife a break from looking after us/take Mom to Las Vegas." It doesn't have to be heartbreaking, just personal.

If it's an audition for a reality TV show, an answer might go along the lines of: "I watch the show, obviously, but there was this one moment when one of the men on it absolutely knew he couldn't get through the next challenge. He was really on the brink of quitting and you could see the tears in his eyes but something made him grit his teeth and he did it. I'll never forget his face, that sense of confidence, like he'd survived a real ordeal and was so strong. He changed that day. I know there's so much I've stepped away from in my life. I just need to prove somehow that I could have a moment like that and not let myself down."

Basic good breathing, done regularly in the hour leading up to the audition/interview, can relax nerves. Practise the following routine:

- Breathe in deeply through the nose then exhale slowly through the mouth.
- Take care that you are inhaling from the tummy and not hunching your shoulders or tensing your chest.
- Repeat ten times.
- Wait a while and then do it again.

Try to find somewhere you can get some fresh air before going in; it will give you energy. Alternatively, if you feel you really need invigorating, find a quiet corner and speed run on the spot, pumping your arms and legs fast for 20 seconds. The aim is to get the blood flowing, not to get out of breath! You will feel light on your feet afterwards and ready for anything.

You should be pleasant to others in the waiting area but don't engage too deeply in conversation. They may and try to freak you out with horror stories or try to sound superior or more experienced. Don't concentrate on them too much – most of them will talk a good game but be disappointing in practice.

Just before you go into the room, smile broadly and as genuinely as you can. It does wonders for your confidence but, more importantly, relaxes your facial muscles thus avoiding frozen jaw.

Remember some nerves are good! It's a sign that the adrenalin is flowing and that's good for your energy and concentration. Mistrust people who say they never get nervous – their eyes will not have the light of battle in them.

As you are about to walk into the room, roll your shoulders back to release tension and 'unhunch' them. Lift your chin so that your head is held confidently.

You should speak as yourself. Don't put on a false accent or try to sound different. Microphones pick up phoney sounds really easily, but do take your time, particularly if you are feeling a bit nervous because the tendency is to rush.

Say to yourself before you open your mouth:

• Take a breath and enjoy what I am about to say.
• My words are as valuable and as important as the next person's.
• I am going to make the absolute most of this moment.
• Don't forget to keep breathing!

Make sure that your voice is not too quiet or too thin; the voice will happily betray unease if you let it. The defence mechanisms that can come into play when you are nervous have the following effect:

• your voice goes higher in pitch and becomes unfocused; it lacks flexibility and sounds mechanical and thin
• tension in the neck and shoulders freezes the throat and weakens the breath.

So, prepare in advance with the breathing exercises and the shoulder rolls (with children, let them imagine they are a cat stretching before sleep, every limb elongating, every muscle stretched, then with a release of breath, it releases its muscles).

• Fake a wide yawn to relax the jaw and take in oxygen (a real yawn often follows which is all well and good).
• Imagine your voice as a ball you are throwing to the interviewer – it should reach across the room or desk to them, not fall to the floor halfway. Practise this beforehand with other people, not so that you can blast them but so that your voice has real energy as it crosses from you to someone else.

If you sink down in the chair or try to feel invisible, that is how you will come across. Be confident in your own body, sitting forwards, chin slightly raised, engaging with the interviewer.

You can build up a sense of your own presence beforehand. Practise at home:

- As you walk downstairs, look carefully at everything round you, what your step sounds like, the touch of your hand on the banister.
- While driving your car, become aware of your back against the seat, the feel of your steering wheel, the framework of the car around you, the landscape outside.
- In a shop or office, observe the space around you, every person, how you move through the space, your walk, how you hold your bag or your coat.

All of this heightens your sense of your own presence so that when you are in the interview, you are used to being aware of yourself and not shrinking away from the situation.

If you are required to speak into a camera, imagine that someone you trust and like is behind the lens, look through the camera's eye and speak directly to them. It makes the impersonal equipment a real human being, one you can be friendly with. A good tip is to watch Fern Britten and Philip Schofield on *This Morning*; they are particularly good at this, speaking directly to the camera as if to one of their personal friends.

In a similar vein, when you get into the audition or interview, imagine someone you are fond of or would like to impress sitting on the side, secretly watching you (your grandmother, your best friend, a favourite teacher). Do not look in that direction but get the feeling that you are doing the interview for them; it makes it a lot more personal and will help you to appear more natural to the interviewer.'

(Miranda Powell, drama coach, BA Hons (Oxon) LGSM)

Last minute checklist

- Double check the appointment time (if you have one) or when the gates open and allow plenty of time to get there without a last minute rush.
- Wear what you are at ease in, though remaining appropriate to the occasion. You are turning up as you, not someone you think you should be.

- If you have too much time and you know that coffee peps you up, go and have a coffee.
- If coffee makes you need the bathroom, don't have coffee!
- Walk, with interest, around the area, practising the 'sense of presence' exercise.
- Listen to your feel-good music.
- Do your breathing exercises.
- Smile.
- Roll back your shoulders.
- Check your hair, zips, teeth, make-up.
- Go to the bathroom.
- Remember, everyone else is just a person too.
- Most important of all, if you go in with your nerves lurking but not dominating, light-hearted and feeling good, relaxed shoulders and breathing well, visualizing people you like around you, your voice flexible and clear, you are able to smile and look the interviewer in the eye, then ... you may even enjoy yourself.

And the result?

'TV companies like to be in control. We like to match someone who would make great telly with a good idea. You can pull out people for a shortlist but Channel 4 has the final say so, signing off who they want from the final list. As far as the production team go, we have to develop an instinct for what the commissioning editor is looking for.'

(Chloe Nisbet, researcher on *10 Years Younger*)

Reasons for being accepted by a programme:

- passion
- enthusiasm
- honesty
- energy
- charisma.

Reasons for being turned down by a programme:

- inarticulate
- no enthusiasm or passion
- difficult and unco-operative

- your 'story' is inconsistent
- hostile and aggressive
- too similar to somebody else.

Ultimately, almost every channel has the final say on who appears in the programmes. The buck stops with the executive producer/show runner of the programme, before coming to rest on the desk of the commissioning editors/network executives. A production team will narrow it down to maybe three, six or ten people (depending on the programme and the length of the series) and then send the tape up to the channel to make the final choice.

If you have gone all the way to the recce stage you will get a phone call from the production company to let you know if you have made it. If you haven't made it through, you may not get a call. Be prepared for that. The researcher or casting team member should tell you at the final interview/audition stage whether you will hear from them if the answer is 'No'.

If, after a telephone interview, you have not heard anything for three weeks, it is perfectly acceptable to phone up and just check what is happening. It may be that the selection process is taking longer than anticipated or they are still casting. If you are lucky, you will get to speak to someone; if it is for a very popular show (like *Britain's/America's Got Talent*) you may just reach an answer phone. Just be polite and state your request briefly.

Some talent shows will tell you that you have got through to their shortlist. That is an incredible achievement, so well done. However, a word of warning. If you do finally get a call from the production team for a second interview or audition, in some cases it may well be at the last minute and you will have to drop everything on the Thursday in order to attend the audition on a Friday. Alternatively, despite being given some potential dates for the next stage, it will not necessarily mean that you will get called for the second audition. That can be tough, especially if children are involved, but you should prepare yourself and them for the harsh reality of TV auditions.

If you do find out that the answer is 'No', keep your cool. It might be worth trying to find out what let you down; someone in the production company or casting department might be able to tell you. But, in reality, that is going to be difficult. Even at the interview stage, the numbers of people involved can be enormous and it is hard for the team to keep track of everyone.

Don't beat yourself up about it. Take the news with dignity and put it down to experience. And then try again!

Case study: *Shipwrecked*

'I worked abroad as an entertainer and when I came back I just fancied having a go in television. So I started to go to auditions. And I was getting the jobs, even when there were thousands going for them. I realise it's because I can make people cry with laughter and I can entertain them … plus, I'm not a bad-looking fella!

I'll meet people waiting to go in for auditions. They keep themselves to themselves and act a bit stuck up. I'll talk to everyone, especially people who aren't going for the same jobs as me, like women, older or younger people. You need to get on with people, get yourself noticed.

Shipwrecked had 150,000 applicants. When I saw it advertised, all my friends said I should go for it and my agent said it would be a good thing to do to raise my profile. The first audition I was sent to was an open audition. When I turned up, I saw all these thousands of people and I thought I'd never get through and I might as well go home but something kept me there.

When I finally went into the first audition, I was with two girls and one other boy. I didn't give them a chance to say anything. I just made the casting people laugh. I've got a really high energy factor; I never get tired. I'm always there; it's in my nature. You've got to have it; you've got to be likeable and funny and full of energy. I turned the charm on and I just kept going.

Afterwards, we were shown two doors: one blue, one green. The green door had about 50 people standing outside it; the blue only three. I got my hand stamped and was shown over to the blue door. We all thought we were going home but when we went through the door, there were cameras and producers and everything.

They ask you to talk about yourself. They asked me who I thought I was most like from the last show. I told them I hadn't seen the last show so I didn't think I was like anybody.

The next audition, you just had to talk to a camera; there was no one else there. I pretend cameras are my best mate. I sang, danced and bent the truth a little. You have to. I've got a girlfriend and a baby on the way; if I'd told them that I wouldn't have got on the programme. You have to exaggerate, make yourself sound better. There's always competition from thousands of others so you need to stand out.

On the island, I was the first new arrival. They said they sent me in 'cos I could entertain. I missed my girlfriend and everything but I was also anxious to be there and get on with it. It was a long journey; from here to LA, LA to Auckland, Auckland to Roatonga, then another island, then a boat trip. It was pretty shattering. I was on my own in a cabin for a week and I thought I'd go mad.

I know what I have to do to impress so, when I got to the island, I entertained. I did what I used to do as an entertainer abroad, I organised games and sports, welcomed new arrivals, set things up – made sure I impressed people and was memorable.

Is there such a thing as good publicity or bad publicity? It depends. One girl from a previous *Shipwrecked* made a bomb but that's because she got her boobs out. She's done lots of lads' mags and stuff like that. So she'll have got money at the time but it's spoilt her chances of presenting. You've got to portray yourself in the right way; you have to think of the future.

I want to be a presenter. So that's why I've got an agent; it's all part of my game plan. There are thousands of agencies to choose from, so it's quite easy. You send your picture along and they'll see if they want you. You can get loads of work from them because they'll get you castings; I've done commercials, photo shoots, television … it's all done to raise my profile. My main priority is television work. You need a show reel and you need a portfolio. Make sure you get good photos because this is what they look at first. My advice – never, ever turn anything down. Be yourself and be confident … without being cocky. No one likes cockiness and they'll see straight through you if you're fake.'

(Adam Child, contributor, model and presenter)

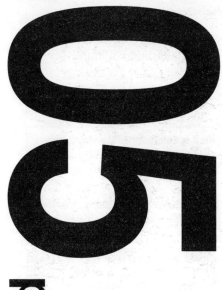

05

practicalities

In this chapter you will learn:
- what contracts and release forms mean
- money – what to expect
- documents and legalities
- how long will it take.

All television is educational television. The question is: What is it teaching?

(Nicholas Johnson, commissioner, US Federal Communications Commission)

The practicalities and paperwork

'A contributor is key to 90 per cent of television. Television comes and invades their life so we have to look after them. We want the contributor to remain fresh to the process but also to know and understand what is going on.'

(Andrew Anderson, executive producer of *Property Ladder*, *House Doctor*, *Families Behaving Badly* and *10 Years Younger*)

Appearing on television is exciting but there is a very practical side to making programmes that you will also have to deal with: tests, checks, contracts, legalities and expenses to name but a few. There is a lot to sort out before filming starts.

The details should be discussed fairly early on in the process so you know exactly what to expect. If you are unclear about anything, ask for an explanation. Don't let the legalities and documentation worry you; they are there to protect you just as much as the production company and the broadcaster.

Testing and checking your details

'As soon as you are cast in a programme, you have a dedicated researcher who will probably phone you three times a day asking for information, telling you things they think you ought to know. But it's not just one way. They are your safety net as well. Ask them questions and get them to explain things for you if you don't understand. If you are a contributor and you aren't happy about something, don't wait until the last minute or let things fester – phone straightaway and ask. Don't fake your 'journey' on programmes like this; you will get found out and booted out. Checks are run by all programmes. On *10 Years Younger*, we ask to see your passport because your age is important; we can't allow someone who is underage to go through surgery. Also, we ask for doctor's letters to check your age and medical history. You will also undergo psychometric testing with an independent psychiatrist. This isn't a judgement on you; it's a responsibility for us and a safety blanket for you.'

(Kirsty Lord, assistant producer of *10 Years Younger*)

Television companies are very responsible now; they have to go through everything in such fine detail because they have a duty of care to the people that they deal with. With shows where you are putting people, quite literally in some cases, under the knife, the programme makers do have a responsibility to test contributors and make very sure they are doing it for the right reasons and that they are sound of mind and body. If they get the wrong sort of contributor, it prolongs the programme-making process for everyone and can be damaging for the contributor. So be prepared for these interviews because they are in your best interests.

Some programmes require contributors to go through psychological tests beforehand. This assessment with a psychiatrist is the final tick in the box as to whether you go through to filming or not. This also means that you could fail at the psych testing, even though you have passed the application form and interview stage; equally, if you pass all the stages for a programme that involves medical treatment of some kind and the surgeon does not think you need surgery, you can still be rejected. It is a very rigorous process even before the camera starts rolling.

'Something that has become an important part of the casting process is a criminal records check. We do police CRB checks on everybody now because we don't want any nasty surprises. A criminal conviction doesn't mean you'll never get on television; it's a question of whether that conviction conflicts with the programme content or compromises the production in any way. We just need to check that nothing's going to come back and bite us. We won't proceed without it.'

(Neil Edwards, executive producer on *How To Have Sex After Marriage*, *Open Gardens*, *The Estate We're In*, *The Hotel Inspector* and *Life Begins Again*)

It is likely that some, or all, of the following checks will be made by the programme makers during the interview process.

ID checks

You will have to show ID at some point in the process to substantiate who you are and what your age is. This also stops journalists from sneaking onto some shows and trying to take part as 'ordinary' punters. ID usually means passport, driving licence, birth certificate, utility bill and/or bank statement. Photocopies are fine if they are accompanying a posted application form. You should be told what to bring or send; if in doubt, ask.

You may also have to sign a form that says you are not running for public office and that you, or a member of your immediate family, are not employees of the network/production company.

Medical examinations

Many programmes will ask for a letter from your doctor to check on previous illnesses, allergies and any conditions you may have. You may even have to go through a physical examination. If the show is to be filmed abroad, you may need to get innoculations. You will have to get a medical check done at your own expense.

Psychological tests

Again, many programmes (such as *Wife Swap*, *Solitary 2.0*, *Big Brother*, *Survivor*) will ask you to take some psychological tests, usually conducted by clinical psychiatrists and/or psychologists (a psychiatrist is a medical doctor, specializing in treating mental disorders; a psychologist is qualified to offer therapy). *Big Brother* hopefuls, for example, will see both at a later stage of the selection process. The tests can include psychometric tests, interviews and direct observation. This is to make sure that you are psychologically suitable and mentally robust enough to take part in the programme. The tests may include an MMPI-2 test (a written exam that screens for psychiatric conditions) and other aptitude or personality evaluation tests (such as 16 PF or Myers-Briggs).

Criminal checks

In the UK, you may be asked to take a CRB check. This gives access to police records and other relevant organizations. CRB checks are becoming common in many walks of life so don't be surprised if a production company asks for you to have one done.

In the US, most reality shows hire professional investigators to conduct a basic research level investigation of all contestants. Their investigations can include:

- civil and criminal court records from any states in which the person has lived
- records from the Dept of Motor Vehicles from any state in which the person has lived
- a person's credit history
- a military record check
- an identity search to make sure your social security number matches your name (all the way through the paper trail of your life).

Searches like these would uncover any restraining orders placed against you, personal bankruptcies, driving while intoxicated incidents, any arrests that have not yet been expunged, divorces and civil complaints. There may also be a neighbourhood-level enquiry where detectives interview current and past neighbours, previous employers, teachers, roommates and so on.

You will have to sign an Authorization to Release Personal and Confidential Records and Information to allow the producers of the show to get all this information. It will be treated as strictly confidential and will not be circulated to any third parties.

A criminal conviction will not necessarily mean you are barred from appearing on a programme. Programmes need to check on your background to see if there is anything in your background that may be detrimental to their show. A few programmes (such as *Supernanny* and *Wipeout* in the US) will state quite clearly in the eligibility information if they do not want candidates who have been convicted of a felony or misdemeanour. What you must not do is lie when you fill in the application forms. If the producers find out that you have put down any false or misleading information, it will be grounds for immediate elimination from consideration.

'You'll have psych evaluation, background checks and a medical evaluation. Even game shows will do medicals; they're probably worried that a contestant will get excited and have a heart attack. We're a very litigious society in this country so the contracts are terrifying to read. They are there to protect the networks, first and foremost. Take your time to read through the contract and trust your instincts. Don't be pressurized into signing anything. The whole process is very stringent but the upside of that is that the process allows you to think about what you're doing and decide whether you want to go ahead with it.'

(Riaz Patel, executive producer of *How To Look Good Naked*, *Ultimates*, *Why Can't I Be You?* and *Into Character*)

Did you know?

Ten different families got through to the final auditions for the first season of *Trading Spouses*. They went through all the medical and psychological tests and the houses were prepared for filming. But then the producers found out that a member of each family had lied about doing time in prison ... so they were all disqualified.

Setting boundaries for filming

'Being on television for a documentary is like striking a deal. As a contributor, you can set boundaries with the film crew but you should set them at the very beginning of the process. You should find out what it is they expect from you so you are prepared.'

(Paul Woolf, development executive)

We have already said that you should share any concerns you have right at the beginning (from the interview stage if necessary), but it bears mentioning again. If you get to the day of filming and you are not happy about doing something, say so. If you are asked to do something you are not comfortable about, tell them immediately. You do not have to be bullied into doing anything you don't want to. Equally, it is not fair to the television company to say you will do something and then pull out at the last minute when the whole film crew has turned up to record it and the programme hinges on this moment.

One contributor did not want the fact that he had been adopted mentioned in the programme; this was a perfectly reasonable request in the context of the show he was going to appear on. He told the researcher right at the beginning, during the telephone interview, that this was something he preferred to keep quiet about. His wishes were respected.

However, if the programme had been about family relationships, the fact that he had been adopted might have played an important part in the story. If he had kept quiet about not wanting other people to know about his adoption, and then sprung it on the film crew as they were setting up, it could have caused a major upheaval. Getting too restrictive can cause problems for the production team and ultimately, they will not be able to tell your story. Be honest and upfront right from the start.

Pulling out of filming on the first day is a bad idea

One of the reasons why reality television is so popular with the broadcasters and networks is that it is relatively cheap to produce – compared with a scripted drama, for example. At its peak, *ER* cost around $13 million per episode to make; while *Wheel of Fortune* cost $8 million in 1988 for a whole year's programming. Big network dramas like *CSI, Grey's Anatomy* and *Lost* cost anything between $3 and $5 million per episode. Reality TV shows can *start* at a relatively modest $55,000, but rise to much larger budgets – around $1 million – depending on locations, casting and production staff, camera and sound equipment rental, special effects, prize money and so on. However, no matter how low (or high) the bottom line cost of a reality programme, the budget is always extremely tight.

For the programme makers, a lot of time, effort and money has gone into getting to this point. For example, how much does it cost to record a programme in the UK? This is a 'How long is a piece of string?' question because it depends so much on the production company and the programme being made. But to give you a rough idea of costs for filming:

- executive producer – costs around £1,600 a week
- series producer – perhaps £1,700 a week
- producer/director – £1,400 a week
- researcher – £550 a week
- runner – £300 a week
- two-man camera crew – £800 a day
- presenter/s – could be anything from a couple of hundred pounds up to several thousands

- if it is a bigger production, you will need to put more personnel on the list, plus lots more kit (cranes, studios, multiple cameras …)
- add to this vehicle hire, fuel costs, hotel rooms, subsistence, any location fees and, of course, all the research and preparations in the lead-up time.

Contracts

'If you're applying to a new series, you always take a bit of a risk because you don't really know what to expect. It's perfectly fair to ask how you are going to be presented. Generally, you should get a sense of how you will be presented from quite early on – by the questions you're being asked and what the researchers tell you is going to happen.

Editorial control is with producers of the programme; it will say this in the contract you sign. But if you are unhappy with an outfit or with the way the questions are going, you should say something – even on camera. Don't be afraid to say how you feel on camera. As long as it's light-hearted, there won't be a problem.'

(Zoe Case, researcher on *10 Years Younger* and *Embarrassing Illnesses*)

Some people can get very nervous about editorial control and how they might be shown in the final programme. But if you study that show and work out how it portrays people, you will get a pretty good idea of how you might come over. People who watch *Big Brother*, for instance, do so because they want a bit of shock horror. If they then want to be on *Big Brother* themselves, they have to remember that this is what is encouraged. If you put yourselves forward for *Hell's Kitchen*, you probably will get shouted at and humiliated by Chef Ramsay on national television. It is exactly the same for *How to Look Good Naked* – the clue is in the title! At some point, your clothes are coming off.

A lot of what will happen is laid out in your contract. Before you go on camera, you will have to sign this. It is a statement of what the programme expects of you and vice versa. As it is a legal contract, it will be written in legal terms but it should not be hiding a sinister purpose. It is there to protect both you, the programme and the network/channel.

Contracts cover:

- your willingness to be in the programme and be directed
- certain rights of the production company, such as promotional use of your image
- the number of days you are needed for filming
- what you have agreed to do for the programme
- the right of transmissions (or non-transmission) on terrestrial or satellite television; as well as the right to broadcast in other territories (such as the US or UK depending on where you are based)
- the copyright of the programme (usually held by the production company on behalf of the broadcaster/network).

For some programmes, the application form will act as a contract between the contributor and the programme. Other production companies will email a contract (or mail out a hard copy) once a person has been picked for a programme so they can read them beforehand and raise any questions they may have with the production staff. If it is a shorter shoot, you may well be given the contract on the day of filming. You should still have time to read it through though and make sure you are happy with everything that is there.

In some cases, you can ask for amendments. If you have concerns, or there are no-go areas in your life (like the man who was adopted), voice that from the start. Don't wait until filming starts. A production team will always take your wishes into account; as long as it does not affect the programme.

For makeover programmes, the production company will usually cover some, if not all, of the costs of the makeover – *but it depends on the programme*. For example:

- if you have applied to go on a garden makeover programme that will be transforming your garden for a relatively modest price, the production company or channel will probably meet those costs
- if you are already considering renovating your house or garden, and decide to put yourself forward for a programme, do not expect to have the production company foot your renovation bill
- in some cases, the costs may be split between the programme and the contributor.

All of this should be discussed right at the beginning of the application process. The details may well be in the terms and conditions that accompany the application form, but if you cannot find any details, ask what is expected of you regarding costs as soon as you get to speak to a member of the production team.

In some cases, contributors will get an honorarium (an *ex gratia* payment) for their services in making the programme. Pie Town Productions, for example, paid an honorarium of $1500 (with $500 for the real estate agent) once all the days of *House Hunter* were taped. Contestants on *Big Brother* will get a weekly stipend for each week that they remain in the *Big Brother* house. Honorariums and stipends are not usually huge amounts of money and they are exceptions to the rule. Most programmes will not pay you for your time. If you cannot afford to take time off to make a programme, do not expect the production company to cover your monthly outgoings.

Any money (stipends or prize money) will normally get paid out after the programme has been broadcast. Contributors are personally responsible for any tax on their prize money.

'On *Property Ladder*, we would try to avoid the kind of people who were more interested in getting free goods and materials or they'd get freebies and then refuse to take them off their budget. This kind of thing wasn't allowed – it's in the contract. If someone is going off the plot and becoming difficult, they can be dropped.'

(Andrew Anderson, executive producer of *Property Ladder*, *House Doctor*, *Families Behaving Badly* and *10 Years Younger*)

Contracts for experts

If you are a specialist contributor (an expert like a hairdresser, a gardener or a dog trainer, for example) who will be an integral part of the programme, the production company could insist on things like:

- having you on first call (another show cannot interview you before the programme you have the agreement with)
- being exclusive to the production or the programme.

The contract you sign is, therefore, more detailed than a standard contributor's agreement.

'Don't do the diva thing. It's never a good idea to demand kittens to play with, a thousand roses of a certain shade and chilled spring water from a particular mountain in your dressing room – if you get a dressing room. That might be fine if you're the goddess of pop but not when you're a TV expert. When you are first starting out, it's never a good idea to make unreasonable demands. We've all worked with people like that and it's not an experience we're likely to want to repeat. The whole experience should be a pleasure for all concerned. If you have three good dog trainers, for example, but one comes with a bit of a reputation, it might make you think twice when casting.

Some of the best people to work with in TV know their worth but they go about it in a very quiet, low-key way. They don't necessarily insist on travelling first class or getting preferential treatment. They can command a high fee and probably would be given everything they ask for but they are very giving and very professional. They make the process a joy.'

(AT, head of TV production)

Confidentiality agreement

Some contracts will have a confidentiality agreement which means you cannot tell people the outcome of the programme until it is broadcast. You may not even be able to tell anyone you were on the programme. A recent *Masterchef*, for example, was shot in September but broadcast in the February of the following year. The participants, particularly the finalists, had to remain tight-lipped until the final was broadcast. You will not be the only one signing the agreement; members of the production team and film crew may well have had to sign one too.

Some producers will build a financial penalty in to the confidentiality agreement. For *Survivor*, the fine is $5 million more than the prize the sole survivor takes home. For the cast and crew members (and anyone else who comes into contact with the production) of *The Amazing Race* the fine is $10 million.

Child Entertainment Licence

In the UK, children who are taking part in entertainment will need an Entertainment Licence which is issued by the child's Local Education Authority. This is usually applied for by the person who is responsible for the production or activity (such as the programme maker) or, in some circumstances (such as second auditions for *Britain's Got Talent*), the parent of the child may be asked to get the licence on their behalf.

You will need a licence:

- if payment is made in respect of the child taking part
- if the child is required to be absent from school for either rehearsals or performance
- if the child has performed for four days in the previous six months, whether or not a licence was required for that performance.

You will not need a licence:

- if the 'entertainment' is school children taking part in school productions
- if the production is organized by an amateur group (like an amateur operatic society), then the organizers of the group must apply and get permission from the LEA before a child can appear in their production
- if the child is taking part in no more than four performances in a six-month period.

If an Entertainment Licence is issued, there is a legal requirement that the child must be chaperoned either by their own parent (a parent cannot delegate this responsibility to any other person) or by an official chaperone, provided by the TV programme.

The licence may include the condition to the effect that they must receive tuition during the event. The licence holder (the production company) must provide an approved tutor. A child:

- must not receive less than six hours tuition during each weekly period
- must not receive more than a maximum of five hours tuition on any one day
- may be taught on days other than 'normal' school days.

If you would like more information on this, you should talk to your researcher or your LEA who will have advice and information on all aspects of Child Entertainment Licences.

In the US, state laws govern the number of hours a child can legally work in television and film. You should check what the individual state regulations allow if your child is going to take part in a programme. As the parent or legal guardian of the child, it will be your responsibility to check with the school if filming takes place during term-time.

Release or consent form

These are usually much shorter documents than the contract and tend to be used for minor appearances. Basically they say that you have been asked for permission to film you and edit your contribution and that it has been explained to you what you have been filmed for.

It is important for the production company to have this document because it is proof to the channel/network that the production company have got your permission.

If you have not signed a contract or a release form, your performance will not be broadcast.

If you are appearing as an expert, you will probably get paid a 'fee'. Say, for example, the programme is about poisons and they need a toxicologist as a specialist contributor. The production company and the expert will agree a standard fee, something like £100 or $200. This should be discussed and agreed upfront. In the States, the American Federation of Television & Radio Artists (AFTRA) set the standard rates. Then, like any other contributor, the expert or specialist will sign a release form.

Case study: Becoming an expert

'By trade I'm a consultant on Harley Street. The [TV thing] all started when I was helping to promote a cosmetic surgery clinic. I became the focus of an interview which got a spread across the *Sunday Express*. This got picked up by *GMTV* and I then ended up on the Lorraine Kelly show doing a three- to four-minute interview. She rabbited on and, when it was my turn, I rabbited on (a case of verbal diarrhoea) saying a lot about nothing. I thought it was a disaster but at least I looked good!

But when I walked out of the studio my phone was red hot: agents, more TV, publicity, appearance, you name it. So I started doing the circuit. I was really staggered at the amount of interest. When they got hold of my professional background they realised that I wasn't just a blonde bimbo, that I was able to speak as an ambassador for the positive benefits of cosmetic surgery. I can be funny and frank or do in-depth debates.

When I first started being asked for TV interviews, I asked how much they would pay me. They gasped and said they didn't pay. And I replied that I had to sort out babysitters, taxis; I had to get my hair and my nails done. I thought it was ludicrous. The channels have got fortunes. Their reply was: "Think of the exposure you'll be getting." So I did. I thought I'd give it a three- to four-month run but I knew I could earn more money doing a face peel or Botox injection. In the end, I decided I wouldn't do anything unless they paid me for it. And they do. If you're starting out in this business you can't be poor – especially if you need to look good. It costs a fortune for me to look the way I do.

They leave everything to the eleventh hour. I've got used to it now but it can be really difficult to reorganize your life to fit in with the TV's requirements. They ask a lot of you. I still find it fun, though. It still gets the adrenalin going.

(Sarah Burge, the real life Barbie)

Expenses

The way production companies deal with contributors' expenses varies slightly from programme to programme but generally the following apply:

- You will not get expenses for travelling to interviews, open casting calls and semi-final auditions.
- In the US, if you make it to the final round of auditions, in some cases you will probably be flown to Los Angeles and put up at a hotel at the production company's/network's expense while the audition process takes place. The return flights are economy and the hotel accommodation includes room and tax only; you will be given a per diem allowance (see below).
- If you do make it to the filming stage (either in the US or UK), travel expenses (and putting you up overnight if you live a distance away) are usually – but not always – provided.
- You might, in a very few cases, get loss of earning for one day but this is rare – don't expect it.

Some production companies operate *per diems*. These are rather like an expenses allowance. There is a set amount for your breakfast, lunch, evening meal, and so on which you will be given for each day of filming. The rate is set by the production company and it applies to everyone: contributors, directors, presenters, camera and sound, runners ... they all get the same. If you have to stay overnight, the production company will pay for that but if you require an evening meal, you will be given a *per diem*. Your researcher, or someone similar, will sign a form and give you the cash for a meal.

Alternatively, you may be asked to present a receipt for your meal to the researcher who will reimburse you. It just depends on the production company. If the production team does offer to pay for your meal while filming or researching, you do not have carte blanche to go wild and treat yourself at a top restaurant. If in doubt about what is allowed, just ask.

Don't expect a personal masseur, limousines and a champagne lifestyle while filming. Despite what seems like big budgets, all programmes are run on a tight financial string. You should not be treated like cattle but it is unlikely you will be treated like a red carpet A-lister.

How long does it take?

'Even a ten-minute slot can take time. It's better to write off the whole day for a short piece. If we do a shot of you shopping at the supermarket, this will take a day. Not your normal half hour or hour but pretty much the whole day. Take that on board. We have to do lots of shots, setting up of shots, walking around shots and different angles. You will be asked to do things six million times ("Just take that packet of biscuits off the shelf again and put it in your trolley. OK, now could you do it again?"). People do moan to me about it but you need to realise why it's necessary – to give different options for the editing process. If you're ever unsure, just ask and someone will explain.'

(Kirsty Lord, assistant producer of *10 Years Younger*)

First and foremost, you will need to get time off work and the hours can be long and demanding, even before you start filming (*The Amazing Race* takes up to 12 days to interview its finalists in LA). While *Big Brother* is probably an exception (at around a quarter of a year in total for the housemates that stay the course), *How Clean Is Your House?* can involve the crew being at your house from a week to ten days; that is a long time to be dismantling someone's life. Even a daytime series can mean devoting three days, usually midweek, to filming; it is rare that it is less than three days.

While the length of time it takes for filming differs from programme to programme, the whole application process, from before the first meeting to filming, can take anything from a week to several months. On a makeover programme that might involve surgery (for the body) or major building work (for a home or a garden), the time will then depend on the treatments that each person or place has. For programmes involving surgery, it is a minimum of seven to eight weeks but it can be ten weeks (anything surgical obviously requires recovery time).

On the other hand, the BBC's *Cash in the Attic*, for example, only takes three days of filming. Having said that, the first 'rummage' day which takes place at the contributor's home is a long day – up to ten hours is not unusual. The second day is filmed at the auction house; two programmes will be filmed here at the same time so there will be another team or family there. This day is not as long as the first but auctions, by their very nature, are intense and stressful. The third day is the pay-off where an assistant producer will go along and film the contributor on their day out or whatever it is they used the money for.

Did you know?

- In *Dog Borstal*, for every one-hour show, there are over 300 hours of filming.
- Each of the 11 or 12 teams in *The Amazing Race* will have a camera crew following them; plus four or five cameras/sound for fixed locations.

Whatever programme you are going to appear on, you should be told in advance what days you will be expected to film; production companies should realise that you will need to organize time off work, sort out babysitters and so on. The timetable will not be sprung on you at the last minute … unless you are a last-minute 'alternate' (replacement or recruit) and that can happen. Then, expect things to move very fast indeed!

'We were told right at the beginning of the auditions that we could be away from the house for a month. As it was, for me, I spent a week in Bristol, had a week at home because they'd shot enough programmes, and then returned for a week of filming. We were picked up at the station, taken straight to the studios and green room. They wanted us to sit in the audience and watch a show which was a good idea because we saw the sort of thing that would be happening to us. Then, at around 10.30p.m., we were taken back to the hotel where we would be staying. I was then told that I'd be on first thing the next morning which was a bit of a shock but nice to be told!'

(Angela Sliman, contestant on *Deal Or No Deal*)

If you are being filmed at home, remember that the crew will turn up *en masse*, probably all in different cars, first thing in the morning. They will expect to use your kitchen and your bathroom while they are there. Many production teams will arrange for a supermarket delivery of tea, coffee, sandwiches and so on the day before so you do not have to feed the whole production team.

Crews are more or less house-trained – taking their shoes off, rather than walking dirt across your carpets, and someone on the team is usually fairly civilized about doing the washing-up. If you are concerned about them coming into the house and using your facilities, just flag it up beforehand and sort out any ground rules you want followed. It is all about being flexible – for both parties (you and the film crew). Try not to be too dictatorial; these people have to eat and make themselves comfortable in order to get the job done.

Case study: *How To Have Sex After Marriage*

'Debbie, my wife, subscribes to a website which tells you about new shows. All of a sudden, one popped up called *Project Marriage*. She applied for it but didn't tell me about it for ages. I was up for it although I did have a bit of a moan when I found out what she'd done. I didn't have any inkling of what was involved because it was a new programme. The reason we decided to do the show was that Debbie and I were so busy looking after everyone else, we hadn't looked after each other; things had got in the way and we needed to sort our relationship out.

We got loads of calls before filming – to check us out, I suppose. Everyone was so very nice on the phone; you never finished a phone call with them thinking anything but "What a nice person." I spoke to members of the production team, a counsellor and a psychiatrist. The psychiatrist asked me very personal questions: was I depressed, was I abused as a child – that sort of thing. Then, a relationship expert rang. She dug really deep about me and Debbie but I see now that the answers we gave provided them with an insight on us. The amount of information they required was immense and it was quite intense for us but the production team wanted to do right by us.

You speak to all these people, you answer their questions – it's a bit like an exam at times – but you have to bear in mind that you still might not be accepted on the show. Finally, we got a call from the executive producer saying, "Yes, we think we can help you." Initially, we thought we would be filmed in about three months' time but they suddenly brought our filming forward. We had two weeks to get sorted.

You have to commit to these things. Once we'd agreed to it, there was a lot of arranging to do. We had to take time off work (I had to tell my boss that I needed 12 days off at short notice), we had to sort out childminders for the kids, arrange for the cats to be fed, that sort of thing. It was a bit of a struggle. Also, being away from your children is hard. People wanted to know where we were going but we didn't want to say so that was difficult too. I think that's the only thing that production crews don't really understand – the practicalities of other people's lives.

The film crew were brilliant. They knew you'd never been in a situation like this so they made sure we felt relaxed; there was a lot of banter and laughter. They couldn't do enough for you, even in your own home. Colin, the director, even came round to meet my mother-in-law who'd be looking after the kids while we were away. He didn't have to do that but he did.

They filmed us at home first, the day we left for London; pretty mundane stuff, really, like me going out of the door with my golf clubs. We had to do a bit of acting in the few scenes; I had to sit watching television and Debbie had to shout at me as she did the housework. She quite enjoyed that.

Then Colin, Debbie and I went up to London on the train. We dropped things off at the hotel and the crew took us out for a meal. It was all very relaxed; there was no talking about the programme. That was the last night I saw Deb for a while. The next day, we were picked up in two taxis and taken to our apartments. I was in an amazing bachelor pad; worth around £1.5 million, it had a real wow factor. They filmed my reactions as I went in. Then they stopped me and said I had to do it all over again. I was really panicking at this point because I couldn't remember what I'd said or done the first time I walked through the door. It took me about an hour to realise that they wanted you to do things two or three times. That wasn't because I'd done something wrong, they just wanted different shots to choose from. It was a steep learning curve.

There was a lot of sitting around while the camera moved about, trying to get the best shot. There was also loads of stuff that they filmed but didn't use on the show – absolutely tons of it. We did one sequence which took around four hours to film and it never made it to the final programme. The ratio of what they film and what they use is incredible.

The logistics of what is involved are amazing. I don't know how they did it. Debbie's the sort of person who always finds out what her present is going to be at Christmas so I thought the filming, with all the surprises that were involved, was going to be a disaster but they managed it.

The crew has to juggle their emotions and how they behave with people they film. They have to suss you out in a very short space of time and work out how you like to be treated or handled. They were always very professional but they were great to work with. If the crew is having fun, then you're having a good time. Neil, the producer, made me laugh all day long; he was one of the funniest blokes I'd met. Colin, the director, was great too. You become really attached to the crew as you work with them. Apart from the surprises and the intensity of it all, I laughed more during those filming days than I had in the previous three years. It was a real rollercoaster but I enjoyed every second of it.

The whole process of filming was amazing – it was something new and fresh to us. They'd suddenly stop filming and I couldn't work out why; then you'd realise a plane had flown overhead and I hadn't even noticed it. I really got into it and started noticing things and began to help with the continuity. You really try hard not to mess them about. They've been working hard so at the end of the day you want to be as professional as you can be; the least I could do was not waste time and to make the most of it.

We were then flown to Portugal. But Deb and I still didn't see each other even though we were on the same plane. We were taken to a luxury resort and given a nice bit of pampering and a couple of nice treats. We had a stylist and were given some clothes to wear which we were able to keep and we were taken out for a meal every night – different restaurants, of course. Wherever I was eating, Debbie and her crew were about 100 yards away. The cameras weren't on us as much at this point. I think that it was a way of saying "thank you" to us for taking part. We finally met up with each other on the beach at night.

We didn't know when the programme would go out; neither did the crew so they said they'd phone us when they had the date. So then we told our friends about this magical experience we'd been on, how they'd helped us and what we'd got out of it. And our friends are looking at us as if we're off our heads and then they asked us why we'd gone on the programme. "We needed a bit of a slap around the face," I said. If you think your marriage is worth saving, it's worth doing the programme. We were doing it for ourselves.

Colin, the director, rang me up and asked me to talk to a bloke who wasn't sure about going on the show so I did. All of a sudden, I'd turned into one of these relationship people who'd rung us up before, saying "So, what are your problems?" He then rang me back later and said he wasn't doing it because they'd changed the name of the programme from *Project Marriage* to *How To Have Sex After Marriage*. That was a bit of a shock to the system but I told him I couldn't care less what it was called, the programme had helped me in the end so it was worth doing.

It was ridiculous seeing myself on television. Up to five minutes before it went out, I was fine. Debbie got a glass of wine and we settled down to watch it. And then suddenly a) you're on television, b) you don't know exactly what you're going to see and c) you're wondering why bits have been left out. But, even though it didn't feel real, we didn't want it to end.

I'd laughed and enjoyed myself during filming but in the final programme you don't get to see that. I looked so serious. I'd like to have seen me enjoying myself a bit more. Also, some people got really upset because they thought that Debbie came over as a bit of a dragon. But I said, "Hang on a minute, it's not like that all the time." Just because the crew film one sequence doesn't mean your life or your character is like that all the time. They're just trying to tell a story in a fairly short space of time. Also, I said on camera that I didn't like skinny women, I preferred buxom women. Anyway, afterwards, one girl came up to me and said I'd really offended her with that statement. That was the last thing I'd intended. People can take offence at the strangest things.

Our friends speak about the programme still; they got a lot out of it. In the end, though, we learnt more than anyone else. That's down to the amount of groundwork that the team did before; they were very caring. It's not until you do something like this that you realise what a great opportunity it is. It was a good thing that we did and well worth it.'

(John Fox, contributor on *How To Have Sex After Marriage*)

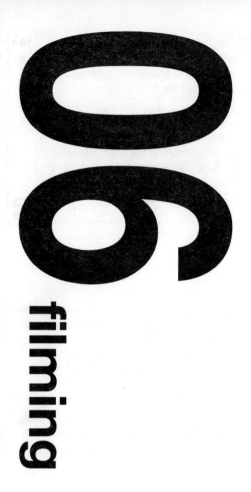

09

filming

In this chapter you will learn:
- what to expect on the first day of filming
- what happens in the studio and on location
- how to behave and prepare so you can perform at your best.

I never miss a chance to have sex or appear on television.
(Gore Vidal, novelist)

Lights, camera, action!

'I was speaking to the director of the BBC3 show, *Fat Men Can't Hunt*, where men are taken into a jungle environment. The director had told a man he'd probably have diarrhoea and feel sick while he was there. She repeated this to his family and to him two weeks before so they could mull it over. When he got there, he hated it because he suffered from sickness and diarrhoea; even though he'd been told that this would happen. There will be lows, especially in a transformation programme. You have to have trust in the process and trust in the production crew.'

(Martha Housden, development producer)

This is it. You've made it! Congratulations. You have been questioned non-stop; you have been briefed about what to expect but suddenly you've forgotten it all; the cameras and sound are in position and ready to go ... This is it! But what exactly happens when the film crew turn up and the director calls 'Action'?

Being on a television programme is exciting but it is also exhausting. You are on show for a long time and your life is not really your own while the crew are there. Remember, too, that the cameras are there to catch you at your best – and very often at your worst – and afterwards, the world and his wife will be watching it all.

But you have been chosen for a programme because the production company wants *you*. They believe you are the person to help them make a great programme because you have something special about you. It can be a bit of a rollercoaster ride from now on but you will get more out of the process if you just go for it.

Filming studio programmes

'For the first five minutes of the first show, I felt really sick. But then everything was fine. I can't believe how normal it became, so matter of fact. To walk into a studio, talk to Noel Edmonds and be part of a television programme. At the same time, although there was a "normal" feel to it, it's a very strange life, especially when we weren't filming. It's almost as if life at home doesn't exist. You could see people behaving in a very different fashion, saying "I don't normally do this." I suppose it's like being on holiday – when you often say or do things that are out of character.'

(Angela Sliman, contestant on *Deal Or No Deal*)

When to arrive

It is important to pay attention to when you are asked to arrive and stick to it. If they say 10.30am, then aim for 10.30am. Arriving late, as we all know, is bad enough but arriving early can be a real problem for the team as well.

Many studio-based shows shoot several programmes a day. That means several contributors are required throughout the day. If you all turn up at the same time, when some of you have been asked to arrive at different times, it means that people have to be assigned to look after you – when they are probably needed elsewhere. There may not be room for you and, if they do find somewhere to tuck you away, you may have an awfully long wait until they get to you.

What to expect

It is a sign of a good researcher and assistant producer if you feel you know exactly what is going to be happening. You should be told what to wear, what to expect and when it will happen. If you feel that you don't know what will happen as the day of filming approaches, then phone up your contact and ask them to go through the steps with you. They will be sympathetic because they realise that there is an awful lot of information given to you and you won't be expected to take all of it in at once.

When the day arrives, you are held in a room with other people who are appearing on the show. 'Held' sounds a bit like you are in captivity, but the team don't want to lose you before filming.

Apart from trips to the bathroom, don't be tempted to go on a walkabout around the studio complex because you think you won't be needed for a while. As you wait, you will get called to make-up and sound; there will be chats with the producer and presenter; there will be dress rehearsals. Don't give the team a heart attack and disappear without telling anyone.

Your researcher/assistant producer will be around and keeping you informed. They should also explain that things may well be repeated (such as walking on, or being introduced). This will be purely for rehearsing, editing or pre-recorded footage and not a reflection of a poor performance.

While you are being met, given a drink, taken to make-up, introduced to the other guests, experts and presenter, the studio is very busy. Before recording a programme, the crew will block out the show. That means working out the lighting, sound and camera angles. Audience-based shows are often one-shot wonders: you cannot call a halt and say 'Sorry, can we do that again?' Programmes like *The Ellen Degeneres Show* have guests walking onto the set, while *The Weakest Link* has people walking off! So it is important that they enter – or leave – from the right place. The director will have set up the shots precisely. If you are needed to walk on, off or around the set, your researcher will take you through what will be expected of you.

Who will be around

On the studio floor, you could expect to see the following production team members:

- Cameras – there can be up to five at one time. You do not have to worry about which one to look at; that is something that the director works out with the presenter and floor manager. You are focused on the presenter or your fellow guests. It is unlikely you will be expected to talk directly to the camera; if that happens, someone will make sure you know which one to aim for.
- Studio electricians – they are responsible for setting up the lighting before recording.
- Sound – they may fit a small microphone to your person. The 'mikes' come in two parts: a small microphone and a transmitter which is about the size of a pack of cards; the two parts are connected by a wire. Don't be embarrassed; sound people have fitted hundreds of these things to people. They do have to get up close and personal but they are doing a job,

not trying to grope you. These microphones allow you to use your hands and move around without having to juggle with a hand-held microphone – a skill that takes a bit of time to acquire even for a professional. Sound may also use a boom microphone. The microphone is held on the end of a long stick so the sound technician can remain out of camera shot.

- Floor manager – he or she is responsible for everything that happens in the studio. They keep in touch with the director in the gallery and the presenter. They are also responsible for safety and the audience; this is the person waving various hand signals at the presenter and crew during a live recording.
- Warm-up – he or she directs the audience, telling them what to expect and relaxing them with a few jokes.
- Presenter – not all shows have presenters but, if yours does, you will get the chance to meet them before filming. They are your guide and will help you through the interview.

The microphones are great at picking up sound – they can record a whisper about three feet away. So remember that people may be able to listen in, even when you are not filming – and don't forget to ask the sound man/woman to turn it off when you go to the bathroom.

In the gallery (the production control room adjacent to the studio) you will find the technical team responsible for getting the programme recorded:

- Director – in charge of directing the whole programme; you may not meet them at all
- Producer – responsible for the content of the programme
- PA – general administration and management of staff; often responsible for financial matters; during recording, keeps an eye on the time
- Vision mixer – controls what is seen on screen by mixing the images from the various cameras, inserts pre-recorded items such as video and graphics
- Technical operations manager/technical director – responsible for picture and sound quality
- Lighting supervisor
- Sound supervisor/operator – mixes the sounds from the microphones, video tapes and CDs.

If you are filming a studio-based programme, you will meet the crew on the day. You may already be familiar with your researcher/assistant producer but probably everyone else will be strangers. Some will have direct contact with you (like the sound technician) while others won't exactly ignore you but will be busy doing their jobs.

Filming on location

'These production companies have a duty of care to the people they work with. People who appear on these programmes aren't actors and actresses; they are real people with real emotions. Television is glamorous but it's also hard work. It's a job but it's psychologically taxing too. I had to do a physical task on the programme that I just wasn't prepared for. It was a total disaster but I had to get up the next day and continue with the programme. I had to put a positive face on to get the most out of it. You have to be a bit of an actress.

What I realised is that I'm a professional. I wouldn't have let down the whole crew. At the end of the day, the programme is there to help you. You have to surrender to the process, whether you trust it or not. Close your eyes and hope you come out in one piece at the other end.'

(Melani Spencer, contributor on *How To Have Sex After Marriage*)

The crew may film you at your home – in which case be prepared for a number of people to descend on you (at the very least, a director, researcher, camera/s, sound, possibly a presenter, maybe an expert too). You will not be expected to feed these people, although a cup of tea or a coffee is always accepted gratefully. Depending on what they are filming, it is not necessary to tidy the place up – especially if the programme is all about a makeover for your home. Otherwise, prepare as you would for any guests coming to your house.

If you are being filmed at home, your furniture and possessions will get moved around. This is not because the crew have taken exception to a particular chair or lamp but because they can get a more effective shot if it is not in the picture. If you would rather something was not touched, either move it out of the way yourself or let them know at the first opportunity.

Getting to know the team

For some programmes (like *How To Look Good Naked* or *Trinny And Susannah Undress The Nation*) the main interview is shot quite near the beginning of the whole filming process. This can be quite a difficult, emotional process for the contributor.

First of all, remember it is not being shot by strangers; you will know the crew by this point. If you are on location, it will be quite a small team witnessing this interview. The producer (or possibly the presenter) will be asking the questions and the cameraman will be pointing a camera at you. The sound man may be there or will have set up his microphones and gone round the corner. The researcher/assistant producer may well be listening but will probably be round the corner out of sight with the sound technician. Just talk to the person asking the questions and try and forget or ignore everything else.

If the filming process takes several days (sometimes weeks), you and the crew will get to know each other very well. You will become part of a closely knit team and it makes sense for everyone to work together.

- Ask questions and be interested in how you are going to be portrayed. Everyone likes it when you show an interest in what they do – television people are no different.
- Be considerate to the crew. Ask them how you can help – whether you are doing something wrong/right for them while filming.

Things can and probably will be shot out of sequence. It can be a bit disorientating but it will all make sense when it is edited together.

Keep yourself occupied

'Contributors have said to me, "If I'd realised how much work was involved, I don't know if I'd have done it." Forewarned is forearmed. People don't realise that you do all of it for real. We really do need you to do those walking shots and cooking sequences time and time again; it's not all magic.'

(Emma Glasser, development producer)

The programme makers want you to enjoy yourself, partly because that lifts the programme and partly because they want you to have a positive experience. But there are times when it can be a bit tiring; there are time constraints; shots have to be taken again ... and again. You can be waiting around for ages, not really knowing why you are waiting. Try and go with the flow, don't lose your focus and take something along to keep yourself amused when you are not required (a book, knitting, MP3 player, crossword puzzle).

Filming is a repetitive process. Shots need to be retaken either because they are not right in the first place, or the lighting is wrong or because the director wants different shots to use in the editing process. Don't worry when things have to happen again and again. On *Wife Swap*, for example, the wives will be filmed preparing breakfast each day. That is ten days of breakfasts. It sounds a bit excessive but it is necessary because no one knows whether this will be the day when something extraordinary or remarkable happens over the breakfast cereal. Two weeks of filming and many hours of tape, will then be boiled down, like a rich sauce, into an hour's programme.

Food and refreshments

Filming can take a long time but, don't worry, you will be fed during the day. Depending on where you are, in a studio or on location, it will either be a buffet, canteen food, sandwiches or a pub lunch. Sadly, it's not all truffles and champagne and it will not be a leisurely lunch. Crews have to keep to tight time schedules; production teams want to avoid running into overtime which is costly (for them) and tiring (for everyone).

Alcohol is not usually served until after filming for obvious reasons. Nearly everyone working in television has a story of when a guest hit the bottle rather too hard before being filmed with predictably disastrous consequences. Try and avoid an excess of tea or coffee too; you will probably feel a bit jittery without adding a caffeine buzz and frequent trips to the bathroom.

> You should have something to eat, ideally a few hours before you are filmed. Don't eat anything too heavy or that will sit uncomfortably in your stomach. You need energy, not indigestion, for filming.

Establish how you are going to be presented on the programme

'We want you to ask questions. The worst thing, and I've seen this happen a lot, is that someone is bothered or distressed by some aspect of the filming process but they say nothing. Then a week into shooting, it's built up to such an extent that they explode and get angry or upset. For the contributors, being on TV is often the most important thing in their lives at that moment, and they are fully focused on the experience day and night. It's not surprising that they sometimes imagine we are all 100 per cent focused on them too. However, what they don't always realise is that we are often working on several projects simultaneously, and possibly juggling a number of different contributors. It's very easy for the production team to miss the fact that something is worrying someone. It's great if a contributor needs to be proactive and prods us if they have concerns. Don't wait for us to pick it up.'

(Neil Edwards, executive producer of *How To Have Sex After Marriage*, *Open Gardens*, *The Estate We're In*, *The Hotel Inspector* and *Life Begins Again*)

Even though you will have gone through what will happen with your researcher or assistant producer, a good producer will make sure you are walked through the process just before the filming starts. You should know when questions will be asked, what shots they will be going for and so on.

You should be told:

- what time you will be needed
- how long it will take
- how you are going to be introduced/described
- what will the on-screen graphics say when you first appear
- how long your segment will be (if in a studio)
- the key points of the interview and the sort of things you will be asked.

If you are promoting a book, event or charity, ask how the programme will help to promote it.

If you have been booked because you have got a 'position' on something, make sure you deliver. Remember to:

- be flexible

- be upbeat
- be polite.

You will not be told the questions word for word. All the team will give you is an idea of the direction things will take, not the exact content. It is not because they want to keep you in the dark; rather they want to keep you and your responses fresh and spontaneous for the recording.

'A colleague was filming a documentary for Channel 4. A whole day's filming had been done when the main contributor rang up and said she didn't want to be part of it any more. She hadn't realised that the same questions were going to be asked in lots of different ways and she thought that the production team didn't believe her and were trying to catch her out. They weren't. They were trying to cover the story properly and create options for the edit. The moral is that good communication is essential all the time; TV programmes are full of decent human beings. It's just that time constraints can make programme makers take shortcuts and forget to explain things fully.'

(Madonna Benjamin, executive producer of *Born Too Soon*, *The Madness Of Modern Families* and *Who Gets Custody Of The Dog?*)

The running order or script

This is a list of what is going to happen, in sequence, during the programme. The production team may refer to it but don't expect to see a running order or script. Again, it is not because people are trying to keep things from you; they want the whole process to happen as it should, rather than because events are dictated by what it says on a bit of paper. At times, the running order or script is not even produced until the editing process. Just concentrate on your part and let the production team worry about theirs.

Do not look at the camera. Pay it no attention, even when it is inches from your face. You have to ignore the fact that the cameraman is floating around, getting different angles, moving away, moving (very) close, climbing on chairs ... all while you are speaking.

Coping with nerves

First of all, nerves can be a good thing! At their most positive, nerves can come over as energy on screen and that makes you and the programme look good. What the production team wants to avoid is a bad attack of the nerves: one-word answers, a wobbly voice and frozen expression. Remember that you are not doing this alone; the production team will have done their best to iron out these wobbles before the cameras start recording. You can help yourself by going through the breathing exercises and following the tips on relaxing before an audition in Chapter 04, page 101.

Whether you are in a studio, with numerous cameras and a large audience, or on location with a small crew, the filmed interview is essentially not that far removed from the first interview.

Try not to be worried about getting it wrong. You are being asked about something you know intimately – yourself. You are the expert on this material – whether it is talking about yourself or a subject close to your heart.

The first few shots, no matter what the programme is, are often crucial because they are setting a scene. This is when you need to make an impression because this is the important part that introduces you to the viewers. Don't waste this opportunity.

Try these approaches to dealing with nerves.

- Take a few deep breaths.
- Massage the V between the base of your thumb and index finger to calm yourself down.
- Exercise – probably hard to do just before being filmed but if there is the chance to go for a run or a short walk, take it.
- Imagine you are talking to one person, not the whole world.

You will have to get used to the fact that while you are being recorded, an extraordinary pantomime is going on behind the camera; the production team will be creeping around, getting better shots, adjusting lights, whispering to each other, slipping off their shoes so they don't make a noise, tip-toeing out of the room to tell someone to be quiet and getting into all sorts of odd contortions ... all with a view to getting the best shots.

This is a new world with its own rules and behaviours. It is a bit like going abroad to a strange country. It may seem very odd to you but it is perfectly normal to the crew. You must ignore all that. Stop wondering how the sound technician is able to hold a mike above their head for so long without wobbling. Your job is to shut that out and concentrate on what you and the others are meant to be doing in front of the camera.

Getting on with your fellow contributors

How you behave with each other depends on the programme, whether it is a quiz situation, whether you are competing against each other doing various tasks or operating as a team. But here are a few tips that can help you get the edge over the other contributors:

- Use eye contact when you speak to them; you come over as trusting and honest.
- Always work as a team member; you want to earn people's respect and you may need their support later on.
- Let someone else be the project manager for the first task; you are then able to watch and observe how everyone behaves and pick up on their weaknesses and strengths.
- Don't be too honest in front of your fellow contestants; save that for private moments between you and the camera.
- Ask the other contestants about themselves, what they hope to achieve – you want to learn about who to trust and who may be in direct competition with you.
- If success depends on a team effort, work out who has the skills to help you to do this. For example: if the tests are physical you will need some muscle; if the tasks are all about organization, look for a manager.
- Become indispensable to others.

Your appearance counts

We are always told that we should not judge people by their appearances ... but that is exactly what we all do when we see someone for the first time. The advantage of watching them on television is that we can make as many rude and personal comments about them as we like; they are never going to know.

The trouble is, while we are dissecting their hairstyle, puzzling over their nervous ticks and wondering why on earth anyone would choose a shirt and tie combination like that, we may completely miss why they are appearing on television in the first place. So the trick is not to do or wear anything that distracts the viewer; people will remember that and not what you *wanted* them to notice.

Take a look at the professionals. The presenters and newsreaders who appear on TV all the time look groomed and professional. They dress appropriately and they behave in a manner that sits comfortably in the programme that they are appearing on, whether it is a Saturday morning children's show or a serious late-night documentary.

You will be judged against their standard when you step in front of the camera so you need to get it right. Of course, the production team are always on hand to help you out with suggestions and advice but here are a few useful suggestions to help to make you look good on TV.

How to move

> 'The lens can suck the life out of you so it pays to be slightly over-enthusiastic and full of energy. Give it a bit of oomph.'
>
> (Chloe Nisbet, researcher on *10 Years Younger*)

By its nature, appearing on television can be nerve-wracking. What you want is to appear relaxed and in control – not a bundle of nerves.

If you are going to be interviewed sitting down, make sure you check out the seating before the recording starts. If you find that it is a soft, squishy sofa, make sure you don't collapse into it; you need to sit as erect as possible, looking alert and energetic – not like a couch potato. If you look at many TV presenters, they are sitting behind a desk. This is so they can lean forward and look dynamic (it also has the advantage that it hides paunches and double chins). You may not have the benefit of a desk but there is no reason to look floppy and half-baked.

If you have to stand, try not to jiggle about. It is distracting for the viewer and can make you appear nervous and shifty. To anchor yourself in position, point one foot forward and put your weight on it, leaning towards the microphone or presenter.

- Before you go on, roll your neck gently, swing your arms and stretch.
- Smile – it helps reduce tension in the face and will make you appear more relaxed as well as keep your energy levels high.
- If you think you are getting too tense, concentrate on relaxing your forehead.
- Television is like a microscope – it exaggerates gestures. So you need to tone them down; they will still be effective on a smaller scale. Remember that less is more.
- If there is a presenter or interviewer, look at them rather than the camera – don't roll your eyes or look away.
- Always assume that you are in shot, even if someone else is speaking or performing.
- Concentrate on whoever is speaking. When they finish, pause slightly and then start speaking.
- Keep your hands below your face and chest and no wider than your shoulders.
- Look people in the eye; avoid excessive blinking, shutting your eyes or looking up, down and around – you will just come over as a shifty and a bit peculiar.
- Don't lean back in a chair; apart from making you look short and fat, it also gives the impression of boredom or tiredness.
- Lean slightly forward when sitting down – about a 15 degrees lean is right according to the experts; it makes you look taller and more confident.
- As long as it is appropriate, smile. Not a goofy, idiot smile but a bright, interested smile. It makes you look energetic and attractive as well as help give energy to your performance. Facial expressions can be magnified on TV as well as gestures. Uncertainty, fear, anger are very noticeable. You are aiming for a pleasant, warm smile with an alert, interested expression. This may take a bit of practice in the mirror at home.
- Models use a technique for a positive smile; they push their tongue against their top teeth.

How to talk

'It may sound obvious, but TV companies are usually looking for people who are articulate. Talking concisely is a bonus too. There is a sort of natural way of speaking in short, clear sentences that is really suitable for TV.'

(Paul Woolf, development executive)

Although we talk about being interviewed on television all the time, it usually comes over as more of a chat or having a conversation with a friend. Despite the fact that your presenter may well be famous, appears in magazines all the time and is always on your TV screen, try not to be in awe of them; they are there to help and get the best out of you. Talk to them as you would an equal; they are not your mother, your teacher or your employer. A sound bite lasts 15 seconds or less; your comments are more likely to stay in an edited interview if you can crack this timescale.

- Speak a bit louder than normal and with energy.
- Use complete sentences and avoid jargon or unfamiliar words.
- Slow down – nerves can make people talk really quickly.
- When you answer, keep to the point. You don't want to ramble on but neither should you give short, one-word answers because then the interview will not flow easily. You need to give the presenter enough time to scan through their list of questions or running order as you answer.
- When you have been asked a question, don't rush to answer it. Let the questioner finish, leave a beat and then answer.
- Follow the advice on being interviewed in Chapter 04, page 115.

It can be difficult. Unlike a normal conversation where you rely on body language and eye contact a lot to tell you when to speak and when to be silent, this is often missing in a TV interview. A presenter can ask you a question and then, while you are on camera answering their question, they may be looking at their script, listening to something the director is saying to them in their ear piece or they are moving to a different part of the studio. Try not to let that distract you and concentrate on what you are saying, rather than what the others are doing.

It can also be distracting if the floor manager is waving instructions to the presenter as you are speaking. It takes concentration to ignore what is going on and to avoid being affected by it but you can do it. Take your lead from the presenter; they will help finish off the interview or move onto a new topic. It is their job to do this and not yours.

- You will be wearing a microphone. So, if you speak, the director will find you and make sure the camera is on you – that is if you have something interesting to say!
- If you are asked a question and you do not know the answer, try to avoid saying 'I don't know.' Instead steer your answer round to an area that you are comfortable with. 'I'm not certain about that …' and then go on to something you are certain about. Don't feel you have to try and answer something you're not entirely sure about.

What to wear

'You are told to bring at least 20 outfits with you. You leave them at the studios, with wardrobe, when you first arrive. For each day's filming, you'd arrive to find your three outfits (for the three shows that were to be filmed that day) laid out ready for you. I didn't have to lift a finger while I was there. Everyone looked after you. You only had to say, "I think I'd like a Diet Coke" and before you knew it, one had appeared.'

(Angela Sliman, contestant on *Deal Or No Deal*)

If you are going to be in a studio, try and find out what the background colour of the set will be. You want to stand out, not blend into the background. You will probably be told to bring two or three tops (or complete outfits) with you; it is a good idea to do this anyway even if you are not asked to.

'Smart casual' is the norm unless you are told otherwise. If you are appearing as a wild and wacky character, then obviously you are not going to be dressed as a librarian.

- Choose clothes that you will be comfortable in. If you look good, you'll feel good and that helps you perform better.
- If you are going to wear a new outfit for the programme, 'break it in' before so that you know it fits and is comfortable.
- Studios get very warm once the lights are turned on – dress for the heat.
- Solid, deep colours, bold shapes and some pattern are all fine. Avoid excessive patterns because they can be really distracting.
- Pastels and warm colours work well in TV.

- A white shirt can reflect too much light, beige or light blue is better; white and black clothing in general can make your skin tone look harsh.
- Don't wear shiny fabrics because it can look as if you have got stains on your clothes.
- Avoid logos because of clearance issues.
- Men – make sure your socks cover your ankles and calves when you cross your legs (and if you are going to cross your legs, do it when the cameras are not on you).
- If you are wearing a double-breasted suit, keep the jacket buttoned. Single-breasted jackets can be left undone but not too wide.
- Glasses are fine but, if you can, avoid shiny frames in a studio and photosensitive lenses on location; it may help to tip your glasses slightly off your ears so that the lenses are angled downwards to reduce glare from the lights.
- Don't wear: sunglasses; large, dangly earrings or shiny jewellery; revealing necklines; skirts or trousers that ride up when you sit down.
- Take pens, glasses, wallets out of your pocket.

Talk to an image consultant and they will tell you that the colour you choose to wear can have a major impact on you and how people relate to you. For example:

- red – a great colour for catching the eye and giving you an air of authority
- yellow – a very jolly, cheerful colour; perks you up
- blue – a safe colour; great for looking reliable, not for looking creative
- pink – a very feminine, gentle colour; all pink makes you look a bit fluffy and something of a pushover (great to wear if you want to wrong-foot the opposition) but it can be used to soften a very severe look
- purple – suggests confidence and individuality
- green – a very calming colour; can help to make you feel relaxed.

'Clothing is a big part of *10 Years Younger* so we do brief our contributors very clearly. We are very specific with what people should wear. Sometimes, you need to be in the same outfit for different days of filming – but you should be told this. If you really do wear black all the time, we'll need to see you in that.'

(Kirsty Lord, assistant producer of *10 Years Younger*)

Hair and make-up

On 26 September 1960, over 70 million US viewers watched Senator John Kennedy and Vice President Richard Nixon take part in the first televised presidential debate. Nixon looked pale and ill. He refused make-up to improve his colour and lighten his five o'clock shadow. By contrast, Kennedy looked tanned and healthy. For those listening to the debate on the radio, Nixon came out in the lead. Those that watched the TV debate saw a confident, relaxed Kennedy and a sickly, uncomfortable-looking Nixon. Television viewers focused on what they saw, not what they heard; they believed that Kennedy came out on top.

The moral of that story? Don't refuse make-up when appearing on television whoever you are. Television is great at making something out of nothing. It can enhance both good and bad points. For the most part, you need to be able to use it to make yourself look good.

Now is not the time to try out a new hairdo or attempt something different with your make-up. You do not want to be worrying about whether it was the right look to go for when you should be concentrating on what you are saying.

If you are a guest in a studio, make-up will get you ready for the camera. If you are not sure whether make-up services are provided, ask before you get there. Don't expect the full spa treatment – unless that is what the programme is all about. The hair and make-up department will make you presentable for the camera and ensure you are not looking too greasy or shiny. They are not there to give you a shampoo and set.

If you don't have the help of a professional and you are on your own, the following tips will help:

- For women – normal every day make-up will be fine. Bright red lipstick can look a bit OTT, as does lip gloss and shiny make-up that shimmers. Wearing lipstick that is the same colour as your tongue gives a natural look.
- For men – a light base and powder will do wonders if you have a beard, a five o'clock shadow, a high forehead or a receding hair line – it will reduce shine and perspiration.
- For both – cover-up under the eyes will minimize bags and shadows; make-up can be used on any exposed parts of the body (hands, arms, neck).

Case study: *How To Look Good Naked*

'I'm a WeightWatchers leader and I was at a meeting, chatting to a friend, saying how I'd love to have a makeover and how brilliant it would be to have someone tell you what to wear. I'd lost a hell of a lot of weight – 8½ stone – and gone down to a size 12. I still felt, though, that I didn't look the way you were supposed to in the magazines. Finally, my friend said, "Oh just apply! What's the worse that can happen? You won't get any reply." So, I went onto the Maverick website, downloaded the application form and filled it in, all the time thinking that I wouldn't be one of the chosen few but for the cost of a few photos and a stamp, it wouldn't do any harm.

The application form is quite comprehensive with very straightforward questions: When did you last wear a bikini? What do you dislike most about your body? That kind of thing. I decided to be as amusing as possible, rather than taking it too seriously. It was really tongue in cheek. I started from the top of my body and wrote things like: "My underarms are still waving after I've gone back in the house" and "My boobs look like spaniel's ears." The worse thing was getting the photos done; you have to have an up-to-date picture of you in your bra and pants with no make-up on. I got an old school-friend to take the picture for me but it wasn't the easiest thing to do.

After that, I thought, "Well, I've applied and now I probably won't hear a thing." I did the application without any real thought of getting on. Nobody was more shocked than I when I got a phone call out of the blue. This girl rang up from the production company and she was really lovely. We just went through the questions that had been on the application form again. She said thank you for the chat and that was the end of the conversation.

A couple of weeks later, I got another call. The same girl rang again and said she had a few things to check on again. We got into more detailed questions: Had I had an eating disorder? Had I had cosmetic surgery? And so on. At the end of that, she said they'd really enjoyed reading my application form and would it be OK if they came along to do a test interview with me?

This began to feel like the point of no return. My friend said, "Oh, don't do it. Don't get into the whole reality show thing. Do you really want to put yourself through all that?" It was a good question. I think that it's really important for anyone considering going on a programme like this that they really think about what they are letting themselves in for. You do need someone to say "Hang on", just so you really consider what you're doing.

It's so easy to get carried away with the thought of being on television, wearing wonderful clothes, having gorgeous hair and so on. You need to realise that at some point you could be seen on national television, in tears, feeling upset or naked! You need to think about the knock-on effect appearing on a programme might have on your job. You have to be prepared that some people might say derogatory things about you. Are you happy to say things on national television that your friends and family didn't know about you? There are going to be negatives as well as positives. Do you really want this? I did want it so I was happy to go ahead. I knew I was going to get the makeover at the end of the programme but there were a lot of highs and lows to go through before I reached that point.

Two girls, with a little hand-held camera, came to my house. You sit in your lounge and they ask you a broader list of questions. At this point, I was down to the last 15 women. From there, the tapes are sent up to Channel 4 and they choose the final eight contributors. I'd made it to the final 15 from 11,500 women which wasn't bad. I told myself that it had been a really interesting experience; the questions I'd been asked had made me realise the bits of me that I really didn't like – but I also knew I'd be really disappointed if I wasn't picked.

For that particular show, all the way through the selection process, I was asked if I would be prepared to take part as one of the hundred testers or in the line-up if I didn't make the final list. So, it's not as if you'd be left out on a limb if you didn't get through. There's a strong chance that you'd make it onto the programme in some way.

There is a big element of trust between you and the programme makers. I would have been more wary of the process if it had been the first series because you don't really know much about a brand new show. Because mine was series three, I knew about the programme and what was required. I knew they weren't out to make you look a fool; they wouldn't be bitchy or try and trick you so the trust was already there to an extent.

About three weeks after being taped, I'd heard nothing and I definitely thought, "Well, that's that." I was gutted. I'd made the decision to go through with it and I was determined to do it properly. You have to hand yourself over to them body and soul.

There's no point saying you'll do it and then drawing the line at having your hair cut, or wearing the clothes and so on. I was prepared to do anything they asked of me. The only thing I wouldn't do was go blonde and I told them that right at the start.

Then, in the middle of my two WeightWatcher meetings one Monday evening, I got a call from Maverick telling me I'd got it. The whole room erupted! I was walking on air. Then, after the initial euphoria, it sank in that I was actually going to be on television, baring all. But I thought, "No, I trust them." I was sure it would be OK. If you have a shadow of a doubt, I'd say back out, don't do it.

For your programme, you're allocated a director, researcher and the same camera and sound man. The whole filming process takes place over eight weeks so it was wonderful to have the continuity of the same team – and you're part of that team. It's especially good to have that when you do the mirror moment which gets really emotional. It's literally like being stripped bare but I was comfortable that the same people were around me.

You do two days a week for about six weeks, in London. You start at around 8.30a.m. to 9a.m., have a break for lunch and then carry on until 4.30p.m. to 5p.m. There is a lot of repetition. The mirror moment took all morning to film, although it only takes two or three minutes of the programme. You're being asked, "Can you sit there and nod your head? Now, can you do it again? Now can you do it standing up?"

The first time you meet Gok is at the mirror moment. He is such an iconic figure that I was terrified. I stood outside the door, waiting to go in, feeling like I was going into see the dentist. I wanted to run away from it but I walked in and he was just lovely, brilliant. He puts you right at ease, telling you, "We'll take it at your speed. Anything makes you uncomfortable, tell us and we'll stop."

There are a lot of silences from Gok as you do most of the talking which I liked; he didn't jump in and put words into my mouth. That's a big thing with this show; they let you tell the story. At no point are you bullied.

With the exception of the surprise elements (like the billboard bit), the production team explained exactly what would be happening next. And at any point, I was told if I felt uncomfortable I had to tell them. It was good to feel in control; that I could stop it if I needed to. I watched them filming the hundred testers and they were just as fantastic with them. No one was forced to do anything they didn't want to, like going topless. They almost treat you like a china doll, something fragile that needs taking care of. You always seem to be at the forefront of their minds. They realise that it's a big thing for you and they never ever lose sight of that.

Filming was done in London and they paid for all my travelling expenses and staying at a hotel. You didn't even have to wait for the money; you just gave over your receipt and they would give you money from a float that they carried.

I signed a contract which basically said: "You will take part in the filming; you get to keep an outfit; if you are contacted by the local newspaper or anything like that, you will contact the production team to clear it with them; you will allow them to edit what they've filmed." The first time you see the show is the day it's aired. It's back to trust again. You trust that the team will edit you in a sympathetic way. I watched the programme in one of the venues where I hold my meetings – along with 60 of my members – from the back of the room! By the time we'd got to the first set of adverts, I relaxed and realised that it was going to be fine, everything was okay. You do need good support from family and friends while you're doing this kind of programme. I'd had three coachloads of members turn up for the catwalk sequence which was brilliant.

Being on the show has been great. It's really helped with my WeightWatchers job. Members will say that they feel they can talk to me; they realise that I know what they're going through because I've felt the same. People, complete strangers, will stop me in the street and tell me how much they enjoyed the show. I've only had one negative comment from a woman who said she didn't like the way I'd come across in the programme.

But I didn't go on the programme for this kind of reaction. I went because I wanted to put myself, my figure, back into perspective. The confidence you get from the programme is wonderful; you understand the clothes you should wear, the tricks to make the most out of your body, the best underwear to give you the best silhouette. You need to go onto these programmes with a purpose. Ask yourself: what am I going to get out of it? What can I offer to the programme? If all you want to do is meet Gok and have your 15 minutes of fame, then it won't work. You need to want to do these programmes for a good reason.

You do become this family unit and we all still keep in touch with each other. I'm in touch with the executive producer and the director; I still get my hair done by the hairdresser (nothing to do with the fact that he's a gorgeous Frenchman running his fingers through my hair!). We're all meeting up – five contributors and members of the production team – next month to have a drink and a meal together. While you have no contact with other contributors while your show is being filmed, the team are keen for you to exchange experiences and keep in touch once it's all over. You're not left floundering on your own because you still have contact with people. At no point do you find yourself cut off without any back-up.

I'd do it again tomorrow if I could. I had the most fantastic time. I loved every second of it, even the down times because I realised that they were highlighting things that we could put right. The confidence you get from it is wonderful.'

(Debbie Onions, contributor on *How To Look Good Naked*)

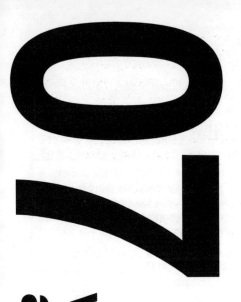

07

what happens afterwards?

In this chapter you will learn:
- about aftercare and what to expect from the production company
- how it can affect your life
- getting an agent
- working in television.

You're not anybody in America unless you're on TV. On TV is where we learn about who we really are. Because what's the point of doing anything worthwhile if nobody's watching?

(Nicole Kidman as Suzanne Stone, *To Die For*)

Once it's over – what happens?

'Whilst we were filming, the show went live and quickly became a big hit. In our second week, we were warned by the production team to be careful about how we behaved outside because we were now on screen and could be recognized. You have to be aware of the fact that you are now on television. People look at you differently.'

(Angela Sliman, contestant on *Deal Or No Deal*)

Once the filming process is over, the production team have done their bit and they will leave you in peace. Your programme contact, the person who was ringing you practically every day for weeks, may no longer be there three months down the line. You will have your life back but you might also miss being the centre of attention and the buzz that you got from filming.

However, you are never just dropped like a stone. Production companies that contributed to this book all spoke about a 'duty of care' to their contributors. It is not just their reputations on the line; they have involved ordinary people in extraordinary, sometimes quite difficult, harrowing, situations and they want to ensure that the experience ends up as a positive one.

The kind of aftercare you can expect to receive will obviously depend on the individual programme. If you are a main contributor, you might get sent a copy of the final programme after it has been broadcast (although it is always a good idea to make your own recording at home, just in case). If you are the neighbour who was filmed for a couple of minutes or were seen driving down the road then no, the production team will not do copies for you.

Your follow-up may just be a phone call or two, with a thank-you card; it can involve medical appointments and counselling sessions. In programmes like *Extreme Makeover*, for example, there is obviously an element of medical aftercare which

'The vast majority of people who have appeared on our television programmes have been perfectly happy. I can only remember one instance when someone didn't want their programme to go out and that's because they were filmed being married and they then subsequently got divorced before the programme had gone out.'

(Paul Woolf, development executive)

involves a doctor-patient relationship. The production team will still be part of this; they will make sure that you know when your appointments are. You should know what aftercare to expect because it will be discussed before filming starts.

For example, you should know:

- if you have had medical treatment, what the aftercare will be
- who will arrange and pay for any consultations that might be needed
- who you should contact if you have any problems
- where to go if you are not happy with the outcome.

Most programmes are absolutely professional and committed to achieving a positive result for both the contributor and the final programme and will have a robust back-up and aftercare service in place.

'Aftercare is important. On our programmes, we go out of the way to make people understand what they're getting into. There can be some risks involved in some makeover programmes. We give our contributors a thorough understanding of what's involved. If a programme is medical in any way, aftercare should also include the usual doctor–patient relationship that you would have anyway – and we see this as an absolute minimum.'

(Jim Sayer, managing director, Maverick TV – producers of *10 Years Younger*, *How To Look Good Naked*, *Embarrassing Illnesses* and *The Shooting Party*)

Will the programme go out?

There is no guarantee that the programme will go out, even after filming, editing, topping and tailing. It can be for all sorts of reasons:

- the presenter changes
- the channel/network pulls the plug
- current affairs (something happens that means it would not be wise or tasteful to air a particular episode)
- it might be whole show; it might be whole series or it could just be the bit you were involved with.

If you were a major contributor, the production company will let you know if the programme is cancelled beforehand. You will also be told if your piece has not made it into the final programme.

If you were filmed at the auditions of a programme like *American Idol* or *The X Factor*, you probably won't know if your 'bit' will end up in the programme or not until you watch it; there are just too many people involved for the production team to let everyone know.

'Contributors should also steel themselves for the fact that, although they may have completed the filming process, they may not always make it all the way to the screen. A poor performance, technical problems or, more often than not, time constraints within the programme's running order, can mean their 'starring role' doesn't make the final cut.

Only recently we filmed a fabulous piece for one of our shows – an extremely articulate and engaging contributor and a visually stunning location. It even edited together beautifully. But because it wasn't absolutely essential to our core story line, when it came to the crunch, we simply couldn't find room for it in the final programme and we had to cut it out. We always endeavour to let every key contributor know when the programme is on and, of course, whether or not they've made the final cut. It would be awful to think of them sitting at home with their friends and family gathered round, waiting to watch their 'big moment', only to discover they've been left on the cutting room floor.'

(Neil Edwards, executive producer of *How To Have Sex After Marriage*, *Open Gardens*, *The Estate We're In*, *The Hotel Inspector* and *Life Begins Again*)

TX: transmission

Generally, though, the show (including your appearance) will be screened but the first time you get to see it is when it is broadcast on national television. Practically every contributor to the programme, including any celebrities or professionals who took part, will not see it before it goes out.

You have no say in editing and no control over this process. But by this stage, you should be able to trust the people you have worked with. Trust is a big part of being involved in television; both for the contributor and the production team.

Open a bottle, settle down on the sofa and turn the television on. This is it! The end of a long, sometimes tiring but also enjoyable, process. You may choose to watch on your own or you may decide to invite your family and friends to watch the show.

Remember: the producer will have edited the programme to make it entertaining. They will not be out to stitch you up but some things may not be as you remember them. Something that seemed fairly unimportant at the time may have been dressed up with a bit of music and clever editing, making it more dramatic or funny.

One of the more common complaints from contributors is that they had a huge amount of fun recording the programme but very little of those moments are left in the final edit. The point is that people having fun in reality television is not as dramatic as seeing people under stress.

How to behave in the 'real' world

Angela Sliman makes a fair point at the beginning of this chapter about the importance of how to behave while the programme you are on is being broadcast. In her case, she was on *Deal Or No Deal*, an ongoing process for all the participants. Other contributors who have been in the same position are the finalists of programmes like *So You Think You Can Dance* and *I'd Do Anything*. You are appearing on national television; at the same time, you are travelling to and from the studios, going about your business, relaxing in the evening – and possibly interacting with the public at the same time.

Even if your programme has been recorded and edited and then transmitted, you are going to be recognized when you are out and about. That recognition may not last forever but it could certainly be an issue while your programme is going out or has just gone out.

Celebrities deal with the attention day in and day out. It can come as a bit of a shock if you are not ready for it. Some viewers feel that anyone on television is public property. They may tell you, rather freely and frankly, what they think about your appearance on TV. Take a leaf out of the professionals' book and be polite and gracious – whatever people say to you.

Fame and fortune

'I feel that people often forget that where television looks so normal, it can actually change their lives. I'm thinking of a *Wife Swap* where one couple expressed what they thought were perfectly reasonable views but were, to the outside world, seen as offensive and racist. They probably didn't anticipate the furore when the programme was aired. The reality is that the camera is everywhere and on all the time. It will see and hear a lot. If you don't respect the risks, don't do it. On the other hand, these downside, negative, candid moments can act as great positives – for the programme and the individual.'

(Jim Sayer, managing director, Maverick TV – producers of *10 Years Younger*, *How To Look Good Naked*, *Embarrassing Illnesses* and *The Shooting Party*)

Reality television has the ability to turn anonymous, ordinary people into stars overnight. You do not have to have invented something amazing or done an incredible physical feat – just being 'you' can strike a chord with the viewers.

For some people, appearing on television is all about becoming famous – a very few of them will be lucky and achieve that desire. *But it is not a given that fame and fortune will follow your appearance on TV.* Don't go into this convinced that it will be the making of you as a celebrity; that way you won't be disappointed. If that does happen, it will come as an added bonus, rather than a natural follow-on. As potential housemates get further into the *Big Brother* audition process, they will be told by a producer that appearing on the programme may bring them insults in the street from complete strangers but not necessarily fame or fortune. The personal release form for *So You Think You Can Dance* actually includes a paragraph that says the contributor accepts that their portrayal on the programme may be 'disparaging, defamatory, embarrassing or of an otherwise unfavourable nature which may expose me to public ridicule, humiliation or condemnation.' Appearing on television can make – or break – people.

But there is no denying that it can happen now and again; it just depends on the individual and the programme. Some people are lucky, like Charley Uchea from *Big Brother*, Omorosa from *The Apprentice*, Tiffany Pollard (*I Love New York)* or Maureen, the famously bad driver who kept failing her test. But at the end of the day, it is out of your control whether that is picked up or not.

'Personally, I just acted natural. I was just myself. I'm wild and argumentative and I speak loads. I just entered the audition and acted myself, I didn't dress over the top or nothing. I told them I was a South London It Girl and I knew that would get their attention. What you see is what you get with me. I just wanted to be on TV. I wanted to be famous. I knew I'd be famous if I got on *Big Brother*. My advice? Be yourself. Be unique and go for it. Yeah. Nothing's bigger than *Big Brother*.

For me, it's made me but it has broken me afterwards as well. I've had a lot of hate. A lot of people didn't like my opinions. What helps? I've had great support from my family – my family stick together. My mum's brilliant but she worries that I get bad publicity. But I tell her that I get good publicity too and any publicity is good publicity.

Endemol have been amazing. They gave me this chance and have supported me. I owe them.'

(Charley Uchea, housemate *Big Brother* series 8)

If you position yourself as someone people are not going to like; your experiences after the programme finishes could be quite difficult. Famous can turn into infamous. However, as Charley said, '… any publicity is good publicity', and if publicity is what you want, then you will have to learn to ride the rough with the smooth.

Did you know?

- *The Contender* was the most expensive first season reality show ever, costing NBC over $2 million per episode in 2005.
- Channel 4 relies on *Big Brother* for almost a quarter of its annual advertising revenues (around £150 million in 2007).

(Source: Starcom analysis, May 2007)

'Fame and fortune? It's a sad reality that for 99 per cent of people, their appearance on television is their only 15 minutes of fame. Unless you're someone like a model or a chef, it's very hard to go on and use your experience and make it marketable. Also, it's not a natural progression from TV to the movies; they're mutually exclusive, to be honest. Just don't bank on a TV appearance making you an A-lister.'

(Riaz Patel, executive producer of *How To Look Good Naked*, *Ultimates*, *Why Can't I Be You?* and *Into Character*)

Media interviews

- If you are phoned up by anyone in the media for an interview, it will be in your contract not to do anything before transmission. For example, after auditioning for *American Idol*, regardless of outcome, contestants are under contract to the show until three months after the final episode.
- You should let the production team know you have been contacted and they will then sort things out, in tandem with the channel, and the press.
- Local press and radio will often follow up people in their area who have been on television.
- Generally, the production company are not involved in this but they can be there to support you if you want it.

If you were a contestant on a game show, it is unlikely that newspapers, journalists and agents will beat a path to your door. Perhaps, if you were part of a really memorable television moment, you will get a second bite at appearing on TV or will be interviewed by the press. In truth, though, even winners and finalists fade into the twilight after the programme has gone out.

'*Deal Or No Deal* came about because we'd been on *Ready Steady Cook*. We had several phone calls from other quiz shows after *Ready Steady Cook* but we'd said "No" to them all. It was when we got a phone call about a new quiz show that I'd joked I'd consider it if there was money involved. We'd just moved into a house that we were doing up and we needed to spend money on the renovations. They said, "Yes, there are cash prizes," so we said we'd give it a go. It was a fantastic experience – surreal – but fantastic. How did I do? Well, we built an extension on the house we were renovating thanks to *Deal Or No Deal*.'

(Angela Sliman, contestant on *Deal Or No Deal*)

Case study: *Wheel Of Fortune*

'I applied to be on *Wheel Of Fortune* twice while I was in San Diego. I went along to open casting calls at Culver City where the programme is filmed. I just showed up along with everyone else; we were taken into this room where there were all these crazy people, trying to be incredibly animated. You fill out a form, play a few games, then you play the game. I didn't get through to the final pick on either of those occasions. Why did I do it? Because, like everyone else watching, I thought I could do better than the people on TV!

They're looking for people who are comfortable up there in front of the cameras, people who can go and do their thing. They're not looking for people who are acting and trying to act out what they think the producers want – and a lot of people were doing this. Everyone was trying to get picked.

I was then in Connecticut when I saw another contestant search so I decided to go for it. This was one of their Wheelmobile events which take place around the country. Thousands of people turn up for these things. Would it be third time lucky for me? There were the same people casting for the show in Connecticut as there were in California. They want people who can play a good game, have energy and a sense of humour. I think my persistence helped too; they knew it was my third time trying out and this time I got through.

When you're doing your show, you get to know all the other contestants because they shoot a whole week of shows in one day. None of us wanted to be up against one woman who kept doing anagrams and word puzzles in her spare time! She looked pretty good.

My show was filmed in Philadelphia; *Wheel Of Fortune* is filmed in different cities around the country two or three times a year. You arrive pretty early in the morning on the day the show is filmed and you have to be prepared for long hours. The production team go through all the legalities and rules of the game with you first and then you have a go at spinning the wheel – which weighs around 4000 pounds and is really heavy.

When we finally got to film the programme, the host, Pat Sajak, heard that I'd tried out a couple of times before and teased me about it. It was good fun. The whole process was really quick, though. It can take around 20 to 23 minutes to film one show. You had to pay attention to what was going on. There were 3000 to 4000 people in the audience; it was huge. Unfortunately, I got a 'Loser' and 'Bankrupt' on my spins of the wheel and I actually ended up only winning $3600.

Would I do it again? Absolutely! It was a blast. I had a great time and, anyway, I need to go back in and win.'

(Pete Mann, contestant on *Wheel Of Fortune*)

Case study: *Golden Balls*

'I was an impoverished student at university at the time when I saw a poster for a show called *Golden Balls*. I wasn't sure that I could do all the stuff that they were asking for but there was a cash prize, I was a student, and for that I thought, "Yes, I could do those things."

What the producers were looking for were people who would make good television. At the end of *Golden Balls*, there's just two of you left facing this dilemma. Do you work together and go home with a 50/50 share of the winnings or do you try and outwit each other and steal the whole amount for yourself? They wanted people who would make this end dramatic and entertaining for the viewers.

When I went to the auditions, the people there seemed to have very exciting jobs or been through amazing experiences; some people had been on television before or were known to a wider audience in some kind of way. Everyone had something very different and striking about them. I wasn't sure that I fitted in.

For the audition, you're asked to make up three sentences about yourself; two had to be true and one had to be a lie. Apart from that, you don't know what else to expect. When I turned up there were between eight and ten people. We had to ask each other questions and find out who'd lied. To be honest, I thought everyone was very abrasive, outspoken and very quick. I thought, "I'm rubbish at this."

But they asked me to be a stand-in. According to the runners I talked to, there's quite a high chance of getting on the programme if you're a stand-in. If people don't perform in the studio on the day or they feel ill (which is quite usual, apparently), the producers will pull those people and replace them with a stand-in. I got to be a stand-in twice. The second time, Jasper Carrott was really nice; he recognized me again and said, "We really appreciate you being a stand-in for us a second time and I'll see if we can get you on."

I spent a lot of time talking to the crew, asking them what they did. I think it made me stand out from the others. I didn't do it to make myself get noticed; I talked to them because they were really nice with such interesting jobs. The people who work there are very good at getting on with people; I think that's an important part of their work. I suppose I was just enthusiastic about the whole thing.

Is it important to get on with the production crew? I would say it counts a lot more than you think. I've just had a call from someone who worked on the show and is looking for extras. He contacted me through StarNow and asked if I'd like to work with him on another project. I think I made a positive impression.

When I got in front of the cameras, it felt completely normal; I just felt myself. It had helped to watch the show before I went on. There was one guy who was playing the game; he'd been in the SAS and was obviously very intelligent and knew exactly what he was doing while we were doing the practice games before filming. He beat everybody. I was watching him when the recording started and he seemed like a shadow of himself. I was so surprised. There were quite a few people who really dominated beforehand and then just couldn't be themselves when the cameras started.

I remember thinking, "I hope I don't do that." I was very focused and very determined. I told myself that you don't get many chances like this. I must and I will perform. I didn't care what was ahead, I just went for it.

In the end, I do think that the producers and runners probably thought I was too "nice" and a little too gentle to make good TV and be on the show. As a stand-in twice, I just about got onto the very last programme in that series. I honestly think they just let me on because they liked me and wanted to give me a chance. I probably wasn't exactly what they were looking for and I think I got in by the back door. They seemed very surprised by the outcome. The guy I was up against at the end "stole" the money, £30,000 in all; I knew that was going to happen because I could see it in his eyes. I didn't fall apart though and I was very dignified. The assistant producer said after the show that it was the best one they thought they had filmed.

I was very surprised when someone from *Golden Balls* recently called to ask if I would like to be on the show again! I didn't think that game shows such as *Golden Balls* had people on a second time. They sympathized with what had happened to me on the show and said they would love to give me a second chance and that it would be interesting to see how I would play the game the second time round. Fingers crossed this time!'

(Selena Kirkland, contestant on *Golden Balls*)

Getting an agent

For some people, television can be a means to an end, a way of helping them get a foot on the rung of the entertainment ladder. If that is the case for you, it may be a good idea to think about getting an agent.

People who appear on bigger shows (like *Big Brother, American Idol* or *Britain's/America's Got Talent*) will get agents approaching them. You don't have to be the winning finalist; quite a few of the runners-up of *The X Factor* have made successful singing and acting careers, thanks to getting exposure on the programme.

Whether you are approached by an agent or you decide to find one yourself, there are certain things to bear in mind. You employ an agent; they do not employ you. Their job is to find work for you. They will have a huge number of contacts and will constantly be on the look out for potential work for you. A good agent will work on commission; that means you pay them anything from 10 to 20 per cent of your salary or fee.

Some agents are also bookers and managers; it just depends on the individual. Agents can be any of the following:

- **Publicist** – generates interest in and manages publicity for their client, including writing press releases, managing publicity campaigns and other PR functions.
- **Talent or booking agent** – finds jobs for their clients. Many specialize in particular areas of entertainment, such as acting, modelling, music and celebrity.
- **Managers** – offer support and advice to their client regarding their career; don't always have the authority to make deals on behalf of their clients.
- **Booker** – usually the employee of a venue or business who gets artists, models and celebrities 'booked in'; they are paid by the venue/company, not the artist. Some US shows (but not all) employ bookers – they are now more commonly known as 'talent producers'.

If you approach an agent, they are not obliged to take you on, it is up to them. Agents specialize in taking on certain types (such as actors, or sportspeople or celebrity lookalikes). Shop around and talk to more than one agent; you need to find someone you like. A client/agent set-up is like any relationship; you have to get on with each other.

- Do they have contacts and influence in the areas of business that you are interested in?
- You will need to send in your CV/resume, photo and a show reel of the work you have done on television.
- When you go to meet an agent, treat it as a job interview.
- Don't hide anything from your agent; they need to know everything, even if you haven't told your mother.
- You and your agent should agree on how you should be packaged and marketed.
- Be professional when dealing with an agent; don't be rude or turn up late. They will not want to send any client of theirs up for jobs if they act like that.

If you do get an agent, you should have a written contract. You need to have an agreement that they should find work for you within a set period of time.

What does an agent do?

An agent will:

- represent you
- send out your details (photo/CV/resume) to different companies and organizations

- have a vast number of contacts
- know of potential work coming up (at least they ought to!)
- negotiate your fee and contract
- network to find work for their clients
- help sort out problems that may occur
- guide and manage your career
- be useful if you have lots of short-term contracts/jobs.

Do you really need an agent?

Consider the following points before deciding whether or not you need an agent.

- Can you do what they do – and save 10 to 20 per cent of your earnings?
- You will be one of many of their books; they will not be thinking of you exclusively.
- Having an agent does not guarantee fame and fortune.

If you feel that you would benefit from having an agent and would like to find one, a good place to start is with one of the accredited associations for agents. They are:

- Agents Association (UK) **www.agents-uk.com**
- National Entertainment Agents Council (UK) **www.neac.org.uk**
- Association of Talent Agents (ATA) (US) **www.agentassociation.com**
- National Association of Talent Representatives (NATR) (US) Tel: 1 212 262 5696

These associations have strict codes of conduct for their members. If you are approached by an agent, or you want to find one yourself, make sure that anyone you consider is a member of these.

Pitching yourself as an expert

'My mate is a maitre'd at a restaurant and they have a strict no *Big Brother* rule. If you're looking to build a career on television, build your area of expertise; for example, documentaries in sexual health. Get well known in your field. Belong to a professional body and let the press office there know that you are keen. You need some exposure before taking up with an agent.'

(Mark Downie, executive producer of *Embarrassing Illnesses*; former commissioning editor, Channel 4 daytime)

If you want to pitch yourself as an expert on television, make sure you are a low maintenance one. You want to get asked back. If you are great on television but an absolute pain to work with, the production team will look elsewhere.

Be pleasant, polite and undemanding. Sir David Attenborough is known for being extremely accommodating and helpful, carrying the crews' camera equipment and, when asked if he wants to be upgraded from economy class, he will reply, 'Only if the crew can be upgraded too.'

Some of the best people to work with in television know their worth but they go about it in a very quiet, low-key way. They don't necessarily insist on travelling first class or getting preferential treatment. They can command a high fee and probably would be given everything they ask for but they are always very giving and very professional. They make the process a joy for the crew.

Case study: Building up appearances as an expert

'I'd written a book about learning to drive, *The Girl's Guide To Losing Your L Plates*, and I became really interested in the whole topic of cars, driving, motoring laws and so on. I felt, for the first time, that I really was an expert on a subject with lots of anecdotes and stories.

I've done a lot of radio interviews: local and national. I'd also managed to acquire various TV contacts and I keep in touch with them. When you contact someone on a TV programme, you want them to know, as soon as possible, that you're not some kind of fruitloop. I send a standard email with bullet points about my expertise and experience. Whenever there have been changes in the law or something similar, I've emailed this CV and some notes about my take on the situation off to my contacts in TV and radio. I also think it's a good idea to have a website with a recent photo of yourself on it, and maybe to upload radio and TV clips, if you have them. I've uploaded a radio interview of myself talking about my book and think it gives producers a reasonable idea of my conversational style.

Recently, there was a news item about getting more people to car share. I got a phone call out of the blue asking me if I'd be willing to be interviewed on BBC Breakfast News about it. I was working on something else at the time, so asked them to call back in ten minutes by which time I'd rustled up some views on the topic – I'd recommend this strategy to anyone if you feel caught on the hop.

I work from home so it's not too difficult to arrange my schedule to fit in with the requirements of TV or radio. However, I live in the South West and TV studios are mostly in London. But I tend not to tell people where I'm based. No one wants to hear about how far you have to travel and how dreadful the journey is. For the BBC Breakfast interview, I had to travel up on the train to London, book into a hotel and be at the studios early next morning. I was out of pocket but I felt it was worth doing for the publicity and experience.

I was genuinely nervous about doing the interview, even though I've done loads of radio interviews and public speaking. I was worried that when the cameras were on me I'd stammer, or dry up, or something equally unpleasant. So I tried to make the experience as easy as possible for myself in ways I could control – for example I wore flat shoes so I didn't have to worry about tripping over in my heels.

The presenter came over and had a little chat with me beforehand. It made him seem more approachable and helped relax me. I took the advice I'd been given (take no notice of the cameras, just talk to the presenter) and it seemed to go really well.

During the second interview, later in the morning, I felt much more relaxed, but that seemed to affect my performance in a negative, rather than a positive way. For example, I started nodding and waving my hands as I spoke, which is the sort of thing which looks perfectly normal in real life, but rather strange on screen. I realised that it's best to sit as still as possible and just let the focus be on what you're saying.

I didn't get a chance to plug my book during this interview but I didn't really mind. It was more useful to have had the experience. I know they want me back and I hope I get the opportunity.

For me, TV isn't an ego thing. I have no aspirations to present a programme. I don't see myself as another Nicky Hambleton-Jones or the driving equivalent of Kim and Aggie. I look pleasant enough in real life, but I certainly don't have the right sort of face for being on TV – I've got quite small features, and on-screen I look like a little pixie!

I did enjoy it. I liked the performance element and I also feel that my opinions on motoring matters are useful and down to earth – the role of giving useful information is very important to me.

TV programmes have their favourite experts who they like to use again and again. But they've also got graveyard slots when the favourite experts might not want to get out of bed – but they still need to have someone as a 'talking head'. That's where people like me come in. I'm hoping I'll be able to move on from doing these interviews for free. In the long term, I'll need to have at least my travel covered or it'll get too expensive. But I'm willing to do my apprenticeship at this and work my way up.'

(Maria McCarthy, writer and journalist)

Working in TV

'I loved the experience [of being on television]. You get a crash course in production: sound, camera, presenting … I was absorbing what they were doing, absorbing everything. A producer I worked with said there are two types of people: "killers" and "fillers". The killers made good viewing, the fillers just filled roles. He said I was a "killer". "Whether you start as a researcher or be bold and try and go in higher up", he said, "I believe you have the capacity and potential for a career in television."

You don't go into a programme like *How To Have Sex After Marriage* and think, "I can get into television." I hadn't any inkling that appearing on a television programme would lead me to where I am now. It gave me a whole new career focus. I started doing fashion styling, fashion shoots and working with photographers. I've now put together a whole new television show concept. It's an intelligent makeover programme and that's what I'm doing now.'

(Melani Spencer, contributor on *How To Have Sex After Marriage*)

People who work in the media are:
- good at communication
- must be able to get on with people
- confident.

Did you know?

- Tracy Grandstaff was in the test pilot for MTV's *The Real World*. She went on to voice various characters in *Beavis And Butt-Head*, including Daria Morgendorffer.
- The presenter, Amanda Lamb, had been a model for seven years when her agent suggested she put together a show reel. Before that she had worked as an estate agent for five years so she wasn't just the proverbial 'pretty face'; she had useful experience which turned out to be extremely relevant for the first job she went for: *A Place In The Sun*.

If you have taken part in a programme, you may find that you get bitten by the broadcasting bug and decide you would like to pursue a career in television. It is a creative, high-energy world to be part of but it is also quite a tough one to break into.

Many of the jobs in television are part-time; people are employed on a contract basis, often for the duration of a programme run (which includes setting the programme up, researching it, finding contributors, being part of the recording and editing process). Joanne Price, the quiz show researcher who was interviewed in Chapter 03, had a contract for ten weeks for one show; the time it took to set up, research and record the whole series. The length of contract for programmes may vary but it is the standard way of working for many, rather than the exception. So you must be prepared for a degree of uncertainty that goes with being a freelance.

With so many independent companies around, there are a lot of opportunities for focused, talented people who want to work in broadcasting. Don't expect to walk into a director or producer's job or even be handed a presenter's role. Be realistic in your expectations – you may well have to start near the bottom, prove yourself and learn the business that way.

You will be up against the full-time media students who are setting their sights on a job in television (or radio, newspapers and magazines, publishing) as well as the other graduates, armed with degrees in a whole range of potentially useful subjects, who are keen to find themselves a job in television. Add to that those people who have not graduated from university but want to work in TV and have a useful skill or background to bring with them. In other words, there are a lot of people chasing very few jobs. However, you bring a pretty unique quality with you in that you have seen and been a part of the television process. You had the energy and ability to sell yourself that got you on the programme in the first place. Hands-on experience counts for a lot – at least you will know what you are letting yourself in for!

Useful places to look for jobs in television

Channels and networks

Broadcasters are constantly on the lookout for new talent and creative people. The channel/network websites are a good place to look at what they are offering and the sort of people they are after. In the UK:

BBC

- **https://jobs.bbc.co.uk** – information on vacancies and traineeships; register your details for further information
- **www.bbctraining.com** – courses and training available with the BBC; also articles and case studies

ITV

- **http://www.itvjobs.com**

Channel 4

- **www.channel4.com/4careers/** – a list of current vacancies
- **www.channel4.com/4talent/** – details the range of talent schemes offered by Channel 4
- **www.channel4.com/learning/** – all about how Channel 4 works
- **www.channel4.com/fourdocs/** – watch, share and make documentaries

Five

- **www.five.tv/aboutfive/recruitment** – Five doesn't actually make programmes in-house so the jobs that they advertise are more administrative, rather than being in production

MTV

- **http://mtv.viacom.newjobs.co.uk**

In the US:

ABC

- **www.abc.go.com/jobs**

A&E

- **www.a&etv.com** – there is an 'Employment Opportunities' link at the bottom of the home page

Bravo

- **www.bravotv.com** – go to the 'Contact' link at the bottom which will take you through to a link 'How do I apply for a job at Bravo?' This then gives you access to job listings for open positions throughout NBC, including Bravo.

CBS

- **www.cbs.com** – go to the 'Contact' link at the bottom which will take you through to a link with information about working for the organization

The CW

- **www.cwtv.com/** – there are links to the CBS Corporation and Warner Brothers at the bottom of the home page. Follow these links to find out more about careers in each organization

Discovery

- **http://corporate.discovery.com/careers** – for more information on jobs

Fox

- **www.fox.com** – go to 'Links' and click on that to find another link to 'Jobs'

Lifetime

- **www.mylifetime.com** – there is a 'Jobs' link at the bottom of the home page, plus information about their internship programme

MTV

- **www.mtv.com** – there is an 'MTV Jobs' link at the bottom of the page which takes you through to a Viacom job hunt website with full details of internships, locations and available jobs

NBC

- **www.nbc.com** – there is a 'Jobs' link at the bottom of the home page, containing information on careers at NBC Universal

PBS

- **www.pbs.org** – PBS is not really the home of reality TV. However, there is a 'Working for PBS' link at the bottom of the home page.

Company websites

Check out the various independent production companies' websites. Many of them have a specific page that lists vacancies and work experience opportunities in the company.

If you are keen to work on a particular programme or with a certain company, it is always worth getting in touch. Phone up first to find out where and to whom you should send your CV/resume and a covering letter.

Use the website to learn about the make-up of the company, who the key personnel are, background information, where they are based and what kind of programmes they make and for whom. If you are called in for a chat, you need to show that you really are interested in and have done some homework on that production company.

Trade press and websites

If you want to work in broadcasting, you should start to learn about the industry. Watching programmes does help. Reading the trade press will be even more useful and allow you to start to understand the industry in depth. You can find out about the people working in it and learn about the latest developments in technology.

It is also a good idea to read through the job adverts to get an idea of what kinds of job are available (and how much they pay).

In the UK:

- *Broadcast* – a weekly magazine for the TV and radio industry. **www.broadcastnow.co.uk** – the online information service (a pay-to-view site)
- *Media Week* – covers developments in TV, radio, newspapers, magazines, digital and agencies
- *The Guardian* – media news and jobs are published in the supplement on Monday and Saturday. Online media pages can be found at: **www.mediaguardian.co.uk**
- *Grapevine* (**www.grapevinejobs.com**) – targeted at industry professionals (from runners to top executives) in the entertainment and media world
- **Mandy** (**www.mandy.com**) – online resource for industry jobs. Some jobs are paid, low paid and voluntary. You can get weekly emails with the latest job information.

- **Production Base (www.productionbase.co.uk)** – online resource for industry jobs. Freelancers can view jobs on offer and set up their own diary service, employers can post advertisements or browse CVs and contact individuals directly. A registration fee is required for full access to the site.

You can also advertise yourself to potential employers on:

- **Start in TV (www.startintv.com)** – you can post your CV so prospective employers can see it. Also, the site gives hints on what jobs to go for and how to sail through your interviews.

In the US:

- *Backstage* (www.backstage.com) – aimed at actors primarily, there is information on the industry as well as details of casting calls (including casting for reality TV). *Back Stage East* is a newspaper based in New York City; *Back Stage West* is a Los Angeles-centered newspaper. Both are sold on area news stands, as well as nationwide by subscription. The website includes information from both newspapers as well as its own content.

- *Broadcasting & Cable Online* – a weekly magazine read by executives of television and radio stations, networks, cable operations and allied fields.

- **www.craigslist.org** – has postings on jobs in TV, film, entertainment

- **www.cynopsis.com** – a free daily trade publication with job listings

- **www.entertainmentcareers.net** – lists jobs, internships and career information for the entertainment industry. Membership starts at $4.95 for the first month and $9.95 thereafter (special deals for three-, six- and twelve-month memberships).

- *Hollywood Creative Directory* – this catalogue has comprehensive, up-to-date information available, listing the names, numbers, addresses and current titles of entertainment professionals from film, television and music industries. **www.hcdonline.com** has further information, including a list of jobs that are available.

- *Hollywood Reporter* – covers all aspects of entertainment news; includes film and TV production listings, ratings, music charts, home entertainment reviews, interviews, award show coverage and other features of interest to both industry players and consumers.

- **The Info List (www.infolist.com)** – a website that aims to share useful and helpful entertainment industry-related information. This includes jobs, work experience, industry information, screenings, casting information and so on.
- **Mandy (www.mandy.com)** – as above
- **Shoptalk (www.tvspy.com/shoptalk)** – news about the broadcasting business
- **The Studio System (www.studiosystem.com)** – data source for the entertainment industry. Subscribers enjoy unlimited access to detailed information on people, projects, companies engaged in development, production, and performance of film and TV content.
- *Variety* **(www.variety.com)** – entertainment news, views and industry events; **www.variety.com/TheBiz** is a business networking site where you can search for jobs in the entertainment industry.

Work experience

Work experience is not just for teenagers; it is invaluable for any job. There are many opportunities in television for focused and determined individuals; ITV, for example, offers over 1000 placements a year to people over 18, in full-time education. Equally, there are opportunities for people under 18 or not in full-time education. Broadcasting is predominantly a young person's world but that does not mean that you will be excluded if you have the drive and initiative to get on.

First of all, you can contact your local radio or television station to get experience with them. The basics of broadcasting are the same, whether you are on a live, Saturday-night show or running the desk at your local radio station.

With some work experience under your belt, you are more likely to be considered by production companies and broadcasters. But be warned, it is tough to get in. Persistence is not just a virtue but a necessity.

Many of the American networks and production companies offer internships; this is an ideal way for undergraduate and graduate students who are interested in working in TV to learn about the industry as a whole. For part of the programme, you will often get rotated through several departments to get a feel for the organization and the industry, before being placed in a particular department. Internships are available in several locations around the country (but predominantly in California and New York) and in a variety of disciplines, such as: programming/scheduling; publicity; digital media and IT; marketing; advertising and promotions; research; human resources and finance. These internships:

- are open to undergraduates and/or graduates only
- are usually unpaid
- stipulate that students must receive academic credit
- usually involve students committing to a minimum number of hours per week
- can run from 8 to 15 weeks.

Other sources of useful information

In the UK:

- **Mediabox (www.media-box.co.uk)** – offers grants to 13- to 19-year-olds, living in England, to make creative media projects (including film, TV, radio, online, multi-media)
- **The Network (www.mgeitf.co.uk/thenetwork/index.asp)** – The Network (formerly TVYP) is all about making TV more accessible. It provides free workshops and career advice to young people. It is open to anyone aged 18+ who is passionate about TV – especially for those who have no experience. They provide free training and events and work with the TV industry to increase awareness of the jobs available in television, to give young people a better sense of what role they are best suited to. The selection of delegates to the events is based entirely on the responses to the questions on the application form. The forms are judged by a cross-section of industry professionals who sit on the The Network Committee. Their flagship event brings in 150 delegates from all around the world to attend five free days of master classes, workshops and career chats.
- **www.hotcourses.com** – a directory of college and university courses in media production
- **Skillset Careers (www.skillset.org)** – a specialist careers information and advice service for broadcast, film, video, interactive media and photo imaging.

In the US:

- **Centre for Integration and Improvement of Journalism (www.ciij.org)** – a good source of resources and useful links for journalism in general, including TV journalism, organizations, academic communication studies

- **Education Video Centre (www.evc.org)** – a non-profit youth media organization aimed at high-school students and graduates that teaches documentary video as a means to develop artistic and critical literacy, as well as career skills of young people. There is a strong commitment to social change
- **High School Journalism Project (www.hsbj.org)** – the project seeks to identify, train and challenge the next generation of diverse electronic journalists
- **Looking Ahead (www.actorsfund.org)** – a programme tailored to help young performers and their families address the unique issues associated with working in the entertainment industry. It supports young performers between the ages of 12 and 18
- **National Endowment for the Arts (www.nea.gov)** – an independent federal agency, the NEA supports organizations that are involved in a wide variety of media activity – including television, film and radio. Go to their website for a list of grants available.

Remember:

- There is no set career route in television.
- Unknowns rarely walk into presenter or series producer jobs; you will have to prove yourself and work your way up.
- Be prepared to invest time, and perhaps money, in developing your skills and knowledge.
- You have to be able to get along with people.
- Many people in broadcasting work as freelancers. That means that they are self-employed, with all the administration, invoicing, and uncertainty that being self-employed entails. You will need basic business skills to back up your creativity.

Conclusion

Television is the first truly democratic culture – the first culture available to everybody and entirely governed by what the people want. The most terrifying thing is what people do want.

(Clive Barnes, writer and broadcaster; *New York Times* December 30, 1969)

TV channels aim to offer a diverse and flexible service for their viewers. Broadcasters want to construct a schedule of programmes to attract the maximum number of viewers. That means creating the right mix and giving the viewers what they want and enjoy. Production companies want to make great programmes that entertain and inform. We, as viewers, want to watch people taking part in entertaining programmes.

And what we enjoy is reality television. We like watching our fellow men, women and children in all sorts of situations. We love to see people struggling with a problem and – hopefully – overcoming it; whether the problem is too much weight, a badly behaved dog or a toddler who won't go to bed. Who hasn't sat at home trying to answer more questions than the contestants in the firing line and feeling really pleased that you know the capital of Peru and they don't? Yes, reality programmes may be cheaper than a full-blown costume drama but they are popular with the viewing public as well.

If you want to appear in one of these programmes, go into it for all the right reasons. It is not just about being famous and getting your picture in the celebrity gossip magazines. Some people who appear on TV win a great prize (a new car, a holiday of a lifetime, thousands of pounds or dollars); others get that new body or new wardrobe and a fresh start in life; while a lucky handful of people will win a recording contract or land the role of a lifetime. But the majority will have to settle for an exhilarating, exhausting but, ultimately, enjoyable episode in their life when they were the centre of attention and the focus of a TV programme for a short time.

Being on television is a challenge but it can be an immensely rewarding one. You will meet lots of different, creative people and be part of a hard-working, imaginative team. You may face tough and difficult challenges; you could find yourself in tight spots and will need all your courage and determination to see it through; you may travel to beautiful locations, see wonderful sights and meet famous people. All of this is possible thanks to television. It can be a life-changing experience that you will never forget.

Case study: *Cash In The Attic*

'The reason I went on *Cash In The Attic* in the first place was because my mother, stepfather and husband all died within a fairly short space of each other. I was having to downsize and there was an awful lot of furniture and bits and pieces that I had to get rid of. So, to be honest, I wanted someone who wouldn't rip me off; and I thought that *Cash In The Attic* would hardly fleece a grieving widow on British television!

It was surprisingly easy to find and fill in the application form on the internet. They ask you a bit about yourself and also ask you to list and describe ten different items of interest. I finished it, pressed the button and off it went into the ether and I forgot all about it.

They then phoned me up to talk about my application form before asking if I would be available for filming. I couldn't do the first date and thought that was that. Then I got a call out of the blue asking if I was free one Friday. When I said "Yes", everything swung into action. First of all, a member of the production team came to have a look at me, the house and my items. The young man was meticulous; he filmed everything with a little camera, got me to talk a bit about myself and then he vanished.

A few days later, they phoned me up again and asked if I would be home the day before filming so that the supermarket could drop off a whole load of food and drink. I was told, "We'll be with you at 10.30a.m." They arrived at 9.30a.m. when I wasn't quite ready for them but it didn't really matter. Everyone in the crew turns up in different cars so there was quite a stir in the road where I live.

It's a very odd feeling seeing faces from the television coming through your front door. In my case it was Jonty Hearnden, the expert, and Alistair Appleton, the presenter. The first time you are asked to do anything on camera, everyone on the crew applaud you and tell you that you're a natural. This gives you huge confidence and so you become a natural. My problem was not to look at the camera but if someone is pointing a big black thing in your face, it's hard not to.

It was a long day, from 9.30a.m. to 8p.m. – absolutely knackering. They filmed everything three times. Jonty and I were filmed talking about an object; then they had Jonty talking but with me staying silent and then the third time was Jonty and I doing any gestures we might have done the first time we were filmed. It was a bit odd but they cut and pasted the whole thing together brilliantly.

It all makes sense when you see it put together as a complete programme but it can be confusing while they're filming. I hadn't got a clue what was going on but that's because it's a completely alien world to me. There wasn't a single member of the crew who was bolshie or impatient; they were just lovely. At one point, Alistair was curled up on the sofa reading a crossword book, Jonty was on the phone to one of his children – it was all delightfully informal.

They reorganize your house completely although I drew the line at having the salt cellar on my bedside table. You are constantly at the crew's beck and call but they're so terribly nice about it that you don't mind. If they'd been any other way I don't think they would have got the best out of me.

The auction day didn't take as long – from 9.30a.m. to 4p.m. They like to film you with someone else so my eldest daughter came with me. On the day of filming at the auction, we were going to meet the crew in Sudbury, a place I don't know very well and full of one-way streets. One of the cameramen had given me his mobile phone number, saying, "Don't worry if you get lost, I'll come and get you."

The crew were very careful at the auction house. Everyone in the auction room was told there would be filming and that if anyone didn't wish to appear on screen, they were to make themselves known. The crew then filmed mug shots of all these people so they could be taken out afterwards during the editing process.

After the filming, the producer asked me to talk about all the items that had been sold and they recorded my voice. This was then used in the editing process. The reveal at the end of the day's filming is completely unrehearsed. You have no idea how much money your items have made for you. I was hoping for £1200 but got £1700. The surprise you saw on my face was quite genuine. With the money made, I went on a trip of a lifetime to South Africa.

We had an enormous amount of fun, especially if one of us got the giggles. I really felt that I'd made friends and I would do it again tomorrow. Afterwards, as we started to leave, Jonty came over to me and said, "You must regard this as a turning point in your life. If I can help you in anyway, just get in touch with the production team and they'll always find me." It was completely unnecessary for him to have done that but it just shows what a genuinely nice man he is.

There was a bit of a to-do over the opening sequence because they had to redo some shots of photographs of my mother and stepfather. But I sent the original photos off and they were returned to me safely and beautifully wrapped up.

When it was all over, there was a certain amount of relief and reaching for the gin. It is a very demanding process but in the nicest possible way. When they'd gone, I could put the house back in order. I didn't mind that furniture and ornaments were out of place but it was nice to get things straight again. You have to watch out because your life gets subsumed by them. But that's why they make such good programmes.

They are an absolute gift as a team. They make you trust them and they don't mess you about. You feel as if you are with friends and that's got to be good. I was very impressed at how professional they were. I never felt manipulated but, of course, in the nicest possible way, that's what was happening. For instance, there was one sequence where Alistair, my daughter and I had to walk through a door one after the other. After the first attempt, Bill the producer asked us to do it again "... but you must be closer this time." So we did it again and went through the door laughing which was a much better shot.

All the crew were doing a job under time constraints but they were always patient and good humoured. If I didn't do something right, Bill would say, "Oh, could you just try it again and maybe do it this way." In the end, I felt quite starry.

The result was that it completely restored my confidence. Those three people dying so closely together had completely knocked me for six. Being told how clever and brilliant I was whilst being filmed was a great boost and everyone was so lovely to me. I thought, "Yes, I can do this!" It really was a turning point.'

(Sara Lock, contributor to *Cash In The Attic*)

useful contacts

For the UK

BBC

www.bbc.co.uk/showsandtours

As well as information on programmes that are looking for contributors, there are details on the above website on which shows are coming up and what tickets are available for the audience.

Jobs and training: **https://jobs.bbc.co.uk**

www.bbctraining.com

Telephone: +44 (0) 870 122 0216
Fax: +44 (0) 870 122 0145
email: **training@bbc.co.uk**

ITV

www.itv.com/beontv

This is a specific link to find out which shows are looking for people and what audience tickets are available: Also:

- **Granada Studios (Manchester)** – if you would like free tickets to see any of the shows recorded at the Manchester Studios at ITV Granada (such as *University Challenge, Soapstar Superstar, That Antony Cotton Show)*, either call +44 (0) 161 827 2740 or +44 (0) 161 827 2070 or email: **audience.relations@granadamedia.com**

- **Leeds Studios at ITV Yorkshire** – for information on tickets for shows such as *Countdown, Win My Wage, Through the Keyhole* and other shows, call +44 (0) 161 827 2740 or +44 (0) 161 827 2070

Channel 4

- If they are looking for participants for Channel 4 shows it would be listed at **www.channel4.com/takepart**

- For information on tickets to be in the audience, go to **www.channel4.com/takepart/tickets**

- In addition to this, there is a special link for the property programmes looking for contributors: **www.channel4.com/4homes/ontv/appear.html**

- For jobs and careers information, go to **www.channel4.com/careers**

- For work experience information, go to **www.channel4.com/4talent**

Five

- For information on Five shows looking for participants, go to **www.five.tv/wanttobeontv/**

- For information on recruitment at Five, look at **www.five.tv/aboutfive/recruitment**

Sky

www.sky.com

The website has TV listings, competitions, information on new series, plus general careers information.

MTV

www.mtv.co.uk

The website has TV listings, competitions, forums and general channel information. There is a 'Jobs' link at the bottom of the home page **http://mtv.viacom.newjobs.co.uk**

UKTV

http://uktv.co.uk

Go to 'Be on UKTV' link for shows needing contributors.

Digital Spy

www.digitalspy.co.uk

Links to reality TV, reality TV forums, news and stories, jobs in TV. Contains good background information.

Wedding TV

www.weddingtv.com

There is a link on the website 'Be A Wedding TV Star' – which lists what programmes are looking for contributors. You fill in a survey to see if you are right for the show. Alternatively, contact: **info@weddingtv.com**

US networks

ABC

www.abc.go.com

At the bottom of the home page, click on the link 'Casting' and you'll get a list of all the shows on the network that are looking for people.

For information on careers with ABC go to **www.abc.go.com/jobs** which lists current jobs and internships.

A&E

www.aetv.com

There is an 'Employment Opportunities' link at the bottom of the home page.

Telephone: +1 212 210 1340

BET TV

www.BET.com

Go to the 'On TV' link and follow through to the 'Casting Call' link which has information for contributors, jobs and internships.

Telephone: +1 202 608 2000

Bravo

www.bravotv.com

For casting, go to **www.bravotv.com/casting**. Go to the 'Contact' link at the bottom which will take you through to a link 'How do I apply for a job at Bravo?'

Telephone: +1 212 664 7459

CBS

www.cbs.com

There is a clear 'Casting calls' link on the home page.

Telephone: +1 323 575 2747

CW Network

www.cwtv.com/

Under 'Events', you will find a link to 'Casting'. There are links to the CBS Corporation and Warner Brothers at the bottom of the home page.

Telephone: +1 310 575 7000
          +1 818 977 5000

Food Network

www.foodnetwork.com

Go to the 'Be on Food' link for casting information.

Fox Broadcasting Co.

www.fox.com

Click on 'Now Casting' for casting information. Go to 'Links' and click on that to find another link to 'Jobs'.

Telephone: +1 310 369 1000

GSN

www.gsn.com

Lists all the game shows broadcast. Good background information. Will request contributors for GSN Live.

Telephone: +1 310 255 6800

HGTV

www.hgtv.com

Click on **beonhgtv.com** to find out about shows that are casting.

Lifetime Television

www.mylifetime.com

The website has all the information on its reality shows, casting information and tickets for shows. There's a 'Jobs' link at the bottom of the home page, plus information about their internship programme.

Telephone: +1 212 424 7293 (New York)
          +1 310 556 7500 (Los Angeles)

MTV

www.mtv.com

For casting, go to the 'Want to be on MTV?' link. Alternatively, go to **www.mtv.com/ontv/castingcall** – this is the section where you can find out what shows are looking for participants or audiences.

There is also an 'MTV Jobs' link at the bottom of the page.

Telephone: +1 212 258 8000

NBC Entertainment

www.nbc.com

Go to **www.nbc.com/casting** for all casting information.

There is also a 'Jobs' link at the bottom of the home page.
Telephone: +1 818 840 4444

Style Network

www.mystyle.com

Click on the 'TV shows' link on the home page to see which shows are currently casting.

TLC

www.tlc.discovery.com

Click on the 'TV shows' link at the top of the home page and go to the programme you are interested in. If it is looking for contributors, there will be a link here.

VH1

www.vh1.com

Information on the shows, news, information and blogs.

Telephone: +1 212 846 6000

Agencies

- 1iota (US) www.1iota.com
- Beonscreen (US/UK) www.beonscreen.com/uk/
- The Casting Suite (UK) www.thecastingsuite.co.uk
  Telephone: +44 (0) 207 534 5757
- Hollywood Northern Entertainment (US)
  www.hollywoodnorthentertainment.com
- Islandoo (UK) www.islandoo.com
- Make Me Famous (UK) www.makemefamous.tv
  Telephone: +44 (0) 208 365 2008
- Reality TV Casting (US) www.reality-tv-casting.com
- Reality TV Casting Call (US) www.realitytvcastingcall.com
- Reality Wanted (US) www.realitywanted.com
- StarNow (UK) www.starnow.co.uk
- Star Search and Elite Casting (US)
  www.starsearchcasting.com and
  www.elitecastingnetwork.com
- To Be Seen (UK) www.tobeseen.co.uk

Also, in the US, the following websites have useful information on casting calls for reality television:

- www.beonrealitytv.com
- www.craigslist.org
- www.sirlinksalot.net
- www.realitytvworld.com

Audience booking companies and information

- 1iota (US) **www.1iota.com**

- The Applause Store (UK) **www.applausestore.com**
  Telephone: +44 (0) 845 644 5678
  email: **audience@applausestore.com**

- Audiences Unlimited (US) **www.tvtickets.com**

- Craig's List (US) **www.craigslist.org**

- The Food Network (US) **www.foodnetwork.com**

- On Camera Audiences (US) **www.ocatv.com**

- Pinewood Studios (UK)
  www.pinewoodgroup.com/gen/TV_Show_Audiences.aspx

- Standing Room Only (UK) **www.sroaudiences.com**
  Telephone: +44 (0) 208 684 3333
  email: **enquiries@sroaudiences.com**

- TV Recordings (UK) **www.tvrecordings.com**
  email: **comment@tvrecording.com**

- TV Tix (US) **www.tvtix.com**

- Granada (Manchester) and Yorkshire TV (Leeds) studios (UK)
  Telephone: +44 (0) 161 827 2740 or +44 (0) 161 827 2070
  email: **audience.relations@granadamedia.com**

- Clappers Tickets (UK) **www.clappers-tickets.co.uk**
  Telephone: +44 (0) 208 532 2771 or +44 (0) 208 532 2770
  Fax: +44 (0) 208 532 2770
  email: **frances@clappers-tickets.co.uk**

- Lost in TV (UK) **www.lostintv.com**
  Telephone: +44 (0) 208 530 8100
  Fax: +44 (0) 208 530 8887
  email: info@lostintv.com

Independent TV production companies

There is no comprehensive free list of independent production companies available on the internet.

The following list will give you an idea about some of the companies making reality programmes that need contributors. After the company name, there is a list of some of the programmes they have made to give you an idea of their style and approach. Independent companies are constantly striving to come up with new ideas and formats that will need contributors.

3 Ball Productions

www.3ballproductions.com

Beauty & The Geek; The Biggest Loser; Endurance; I Know My Kid's A Star; Age Of Love; For Love Or Money; The PickUp Artist; Super Group; Unan1mous; Pet Finder; Turning 40

1600 Rosecrans Avenue
Bldg 7, 2nd floor
Manhattan Beach
CA 90266
Telephone: +1 310 727 3337

Click on the 'Casting' link on the website to find out which shows are looking for contributors. Application forms can be downloaded here.

12 Yard Productions

www.12yard.com

In It To Win It; Eggheads; Three's A Crowd; The Village Show; Dirty Money; Double Cross; Men Are Better Than Women; Here Comes The Sun; Who Dares Wins; Without Prejudice; Beg, Borrow Or Steal

10 Livonia Street
London
W1F 8AF
Telephone: +44 (0) 207 432 2929
Fax: +44 (0) 207 439 2037

Application forms for the shows that are recruiting for contributors can be found on the individual programme pages on the website.

44 Blue Productions

www.44blue.com

Split Ends; Made Of Honour; A&E Design Show; Small Shots; What Should You Do?

4040 Vineland Avenue, Suite 105
Studio City
CA 91604
Telephone: +1 818 760 4442
Fax: +1 818 760 1509
email: **reception@44blue.com**

There is a 'Casting' link with all the information on shows looking for people.

Actual Reality Pictures

www.arp.tv

Greatest American Dog; 30 Days; Greenovate; Flip That House

672 West Sunset Blvd, Suite 350
Los Angeles
CA 900028
Telephone: +1 310 202 1272
Fax: +1 310 202 1502
email: **questions@arp.tv**
jobs: **arpjobs2007@arp.tv**

Betty

www.betty.co.uk

Arrange Me A Marriage; Spendaholics; Freaky Eaters; Outrageous Wasters

The Heal's Building
8 Alfred Mews
London
W1T 7AA
Telephone: +44 (0) 207 290 0660
Fax: +44 (0) 207 290 0679

For jobs and careers, send your CV and a covering note to: **youneedme@betty.co.uk**

Bunim Murray

www.bunim-murray.com

The Real World; The Bad Girls' Club; Road Rules; Starting Over

6007 Sepulveda Blvd
Van Nuys
CA 91411
Telephone: +1 818 756 5150
Fax: +1 818 756 5140

Very clear links at the top of the home page to 'Casting' and 'Jobs'.

Diverse Production

www.diverse.tv

Badger Or Bust; 14 Alone; Tribal Wives; Sex With Your Ex; Operatunity; Ballet Hoo; Be A Grand Prix Driver; Beyond Boundaries

6–12 Gorleston Street
London
W14 8XS
Telephone: +44 (0) 207 603 4567
Fax: +44 (0) 207 603 2148

There is a 'Jobs' page on the website. You can forward your details by emailing your CV to **careers@diverse.tv**. Make sure you state the position you require in the subject heading.

Endemol

www.endemoluk.com

Endemol is one of Britain's largest independent production companies, incorporating Brighter Pictures (*Big Brother)*, Cheetah Television (*Can Fat Teens Hunt?*; *Deal Or No Deal; Ready Steady Cook; Supersize vs Superskinny)* and Initial (*Coleen's Real Women; Golden Balls; 1 vs 100)*

Endemol UK
Shepherds Studios – Central
Charecroft Way
Shepherds Bush
London
W14 0EE

Telephone: + 44 (0) 870 333 1700
www.beonendemolshows.co.uk – you will have to register for access to this website.

- Anyone interested in work experience should email a CV, covering letter and details of their course to: **work.experience@endemoluk.com**
- If you are interested in working as a runner for Endemol UK, email your CV and covering letter to: **runners@endemoluk.com**

Endemol US

www.endemolusa.tv

Deal Or No Deal; 1 vs 100; Fear Factor; Extreme Makeover – Home Edition; Big Brother; Bachelor; Show Me The Money; The One; Making A Music Star; Set For Life; Exposed; Kid Nation; Midnight Money Madness; Vas O No Vas)

Endemol USA
9255 W Sunset Blvd
Suite 1100
CA 90069
Telephone: +1 310 860 9914

On the website under 'Contact Us', there is a link for 'Submissions' which takes you to 'Submit a show idea' or 'Submit for casting'. Go to the 'Work with us' link if you are interested in a job (scripted, non-scripted, digital media, Latino dept).

Fever Media

www.fevermedia.co.uk

Fortune; Million Pound Giveaway; No Place Like Home; The People's Quiz

Development Office
Clearwater Yard
2nd level
35 Inverness Street
London
NW1 7NB
Telephone: +44 (0) 207 428 5760
Fax: +44 (0) 207 267 3730
email: **tamsin.foyle@fevermedia.co.uk** (general enquiries)

Go to the 'Jobs at Fever' link for more information on careers and traineeships.

Flame Television

www.flametv.co.uk

Don't Get Done, Get Dom

6–9 Cynthia Street
London
N1 9JF
Telephone: +44 (0) 207 713 6868
Fax: +44 (0) 207 713 6999
email: **contact@flametv.co.uk**

If you have an original idea for television, you are encouraged to contact the company via the above email. There is a 'Jobs' link on the website. Occasionally Flame TV offer work experience and short-term contracts for general office runners and graduate researchers; contact details are on this page.

Freeform Productions

A Place In The Sun: Home Or Away

15th floor
111 Piccadilly
Manchester
M1 2HY
Telephone: +44 (0) 161 235 6578
Fax: +44 (0) 161 236 2920

email: **[name]@fftv.co.uk** (there will be a specific name of a person for this email address when they are looking for contributors).

Granada Productions

www.granadamedia.com

Hell's Kitchen; Trinny And Susannah Undress The Nation; Countdown; Brainiac; Jeremy Kyle; 60 Minute Makeover; Come Dine With Me; Be Our Guest

The London Television Centre
Upper Ground
London
SE1 9LT
Telephone: +44 (0) 207 620 1620

Granada Productions uses the name ITV Productions when making programmes for the ITV family of channels.

Granada America

www.granadaamerica.com

Nanny 911; Hell's Kitchen; Room Raiders; The First 48; Hit Me Baby One More Time

Los Angeles office
15303 Ventura Boulevard
Building C, Suite 800
Sherman Oaks
CA 91403
Telephone: +1 818 455 4600
            +1 212 905 1700 (New York office)

There are no direct links for casting on this site; instead, you need to go to the programme or network sites. For example, the official site of *Hell's Kitchen* (Fox) will say if they are casting for the show. You should email **hkcasting@granadaprod.com** for further information on appearing on *Hell's Kitchen*.

Hybrid Films

www.hybridfilms.tv

Dog The Bounty Hunter; Family Plots; Take This Job; King Of Cars; Parking Wars; It's A Living

99 University Place
New York
NY 10003
Telephone: +1 212 228 1020

Go to the 'Contact Us' link where you get three options:

- Think your life is fascinating enough to be on television? email: **Development@hybridfilms.tv**

- To learn more about Hybrid Films email: **Info@hybridfilms.tv**

- Want to submit your resume to Hybrid? Then email: **Jobs@hybridfilms.tv**

IWC Media (part of the RDF Group)

www.iwcmedia.co.uk

Survival Of The Richest; No Sex Please We're Teenagers; Relocation, Relocation; Secrets Of An Interior Designer

St George's Studio
93 St George's Road
Glasgow
G3 6JA
Telephone: +44 (0) 141 353 3222

If you are interested in working for IWC Media, contact **cvsglasgow@iwcmedia.co.uk** or **cvslondon@iwcmedia.co.uk**

Landmark Films

www.landmarkfilms.com

Animal Addicts; Fat Pets; Beat It; Britain's Weirdest Phobias; The Angriest Men In Britain; The Biggest Tarts In Britain

11 Evelyn Court
267b Cowley Road
Oxford
OX4 1GY
Telephone: +44 (0) 1865 297220
Fax: +44 (0) 1865 203044
email: **information@landmarkfilms.com**

There is an email link to send your CV to: **cv@landmarkfilms.com**

Leopard Films

www.leopardfilms.com

Cash In The Attic; Car Booty; B&B The Best; Natural Born Dealers; Money Spinners

1–3 St Peters Street
Islington
London
N1 8JD
Telephone: +44 (0) 870 420 4232
Fax: +44 (0) 870 443 6099
email: **enquiry@leopardfilms.com**

Go to the 'Apply' link if you want to be on one of their shows. For jobs at Leopard, go to the 'Contact' page where you will find a 'Click here to send us your CV' link.

Lion Television

www.liontv.co.uk

Castaway; Homes Under The Hammer; Dealing With Dickenson; Fashion House; Let Me Entertain You; Vegas Virgins; Send Them Packing; Playing It Straight

Lion Television (London)
Lion House
26 Paddenswick Road
London W6 0UB
Telephone: +44 (0) 20 8846 2000
Fax: +44 (0) 20 8846 2001

Lion Television (Scotland)
14 Royal Crescent
Glasgow
G3 7SL
Telephone: 44 (0) 141 331 0450
Fax: +44 (0) 141 331 0451

Go to the 'Recuitment' link for more information on jobs, work experience and internships at the company.

LMNO Productions

wwwlmnotv.com

I Wanna Be A Soapstar; Boot Camp; Wickedly Perfect; Race To The Altar; Fit To Live; Fire Me ... Please; Man vs Beast 1 & 2; Over Your Head; Double Or Nothing

15821 Ventura Blvd, Suite 320
Encino
CA 91436
Telephone: +1 818 380 8000

There is a 'Be on TV' link with all the information and details on shows looking for contributors.

Magical Elves Inc

www.magicalelves.com

Bands On The Run; Project Greenlight; Project Runway; Top Chef; Treasure Hunters; Last Comic Standing

General information: **info@magicalelves.com**

For job information: **jobs@magicalelves.com**

For internships: **intern@magicalelves.com**

If they are looking to cast people, the information will be on the home page: 'Now Casting ...'

Mark Burnett Productions

Survivor; The Apprentice (US); Are You Smarter Than a Fifth Grader?; My Dad Is Better Than Your Dad; The Restaurant; The Casino; On The Lot; Amne$ia; The Contender; Rock Star

640 N Sepulveda Blvd
Los Angeles
CA 90049
Telephone: +1 310 903 5400
Fax: +1 310 903 5555

For information on casting for programmes, go to the official programme websites, via the network sites.

Maverick TV

www.mavericktv.co.uk

How To Look Good Naked; Bizarre ER; 10 Years Younger; Embarrassing Illnesses; The Shooting Party

Maverick Birmingham
Progress Works
Heath Mill Lane
Birmingham
B9 4AL
Telephone: +44 (0) 121 771 1812
Fax: +44 (0) 121 771 1550
email: **mail@mavericktv.co.uk**

Maverick London
40 Churchway
London
NW1 1LW
Telephone: +44 (0) 207 383 2727
Fax: +44 (0) 207 874 6635
email: **mail@mavericktv.co.uk**

Go to their 'Be on TV' page for information, application forms and details about up-and-coming shows. For jobs, go to the 'About Us' page and you will see a link to 'Jobs at Maverick' which has information on applying to Maverick and a list of relevant email addresses, depending on the type of job or work experience you are looking for.

Mentorn

www.mentorn.tv

The Boy Who Gave Birth To His Twin; Half Ton Man; Robot Wars; Diet On The Dance Floor

Elsinore House
77 Fulham Palace Road
London
W6 8JA
Telephone: +44 (0) 207 258 6700
Fax: +44 (0) 207 258 6888
email: **beontv@mentorn.tv**

On Mentorn's website, go to the 'Got An Idea?' link. If you think you've got an idea or story that would make a great TV programme, you can contact them. If they are looking for contributors, they will list them on the website with email links to the relevant person (or send an email to **beontv@mentorn.tv**). If you think you would make a great presenter, you can contact them on this email address as well.

Optomen Television

www.optomen.com

Ramsey's Kitchen Nightmares; Mary Queen Of Shops; Food Poker; You're Not The Man I Married; Crazy Drivers; If You Can't Stand the Heat

1 Valentine Place
London
SE1 8QH
Telephone: +44 (0) 207 967 1234

Go to the 'Shows – In Production' link to see which shows are looking for contributors. Go to 'About Us' and you will find a list of jobs with the relevant email address so you can send in your CV.

Optomen Television USA

www.optomenusa.com
72 Spring St, Room 1002
New York
NY 10012–4019
Telephone: + 1 212 431 4361

If you have any questions, contact: **casting@optomenusa.com**

Pie Town Productions

www.pietown.tv

24 Hour Design; Fantasy Wedding In a Week; Color Correction; Landscapers Challenge; Good Buy/Bad Buy; My House Is Worth What?; Design On A Dime; House Hunters; Rate My Space

Los Angeles Office
Pie Town Productions
5433 Laurel Canyon Blvd
North Hollywood
CA 91607
Telephone: +1 818 255 9300
Fax: +1 818 255 9333
General questions, email: **pietown@pietown.tv**

Chicago Office
Pie Town Productions
1438 West Kinzie Street, Suite 300
Chicago
IL 60622
Telephone: +1 312 229 1400
Fax: +1 312 229 1401
General questions, email: **ptchicago@pietown.tv**

Go to 'Get in Touch' for address, phone and email details. There are individual email addresses for specific shows. The same link will take you to information on jobs at Pie Town Productions.

'Be on TV' link tells you the company's casting needs: 'Urgent casting' and 'Ongoing casting'. There is a comprehensive FAQ section for people who are interested in applying to be on a show (for example, how long it takes, what to wear, the number of people involved and so on).

Pink Sneakers

www.pinksneakers.net

My Big Fat Redneck Wedding; Hogan Knows Best; I Want A Famous Face; True Life

1000 Colour Place
Apopka
Fl 32703
Telephone: +1 407 464 2080
Fax: +1 407 464 2081
email: **info@pinksneakers.net**

There is an 'Our Casting' and a 'Get A Job' link on the home page. For job information, email: **hr@pinksneakers.net**

Prospect Pictures

www.prospect-uk.com

Take Away My Takeaway; Don't Just Dream It; Under One Roof; House Price Challenge

Wandsworth Plain
London
SW18 1ET
Telephone: +44 (0) 207 636 1234
Fax: +44 (0) 207 636 1236
email: **info@prospect-uk.com**

If you want to be part of their team send your CV with a covering letter to the address above or to: **Careers@prospect-uk.com**

RDF Television

www.rdftelevision.com

Shipwrecked; Ladette To Lady; Wife Swap; Anthea Turner; Perfect Housewife

The Gloucester Building
Kensington Village
Avonmore Road
London
W14 8RF
Telephone: +44 (0) 207 013 4000
Fax: +44 (0) 207 013 4001
Email: **contactus@rdftelevision.com**

You can log in as a user and go to **www.meontv.co.uk**

RDF US

www.rdfusa.com

*Wife Swap, How To Look Good Naked (*with Maverick TV*); Don't Forget The Lyrics*

Telephone: +1 310 460 4490
email: **contactus@rdfusa.com**

Reef Television

www.reef.tv

Sun, Sea And Bargain Spotting; Trash to Cash; Buy It, Sell It, Bank It

3rd Floor
Wellington House
8 Upper St Martin's Lane
London
WC2H 9DL
Telephone: +44 (0) 207 836 8595
Fax: +44 (0) 207 836 8596
email: **mail@reeftv.com** (general enquiries)

Go to the 'Productions' page to find out more about what programmes are looking for contributors. For job enquiries, email: **work@reeftv.com**

Renegade Pictures

www.renegadepictures.co.uk

Don't Tell The Bride

3–4 Portland Mews
London
W1F 8JF
Telephone: +44 (0) 207 479 4200
Fax: +44 (0) 207 494 9134
email: **info@renegadepictures.co.uk**

Go to the 'Productions' page to find out which programmes are looking for contributors.

Ricochet

www.ricochet.co.uk

Supernanny; Living In The Sun; No Going Back; Kitchen Millionaire; It's Me Or The Dog

Pacific House
126 Dyke Road
Brighton
BN1 3TE
Telephone: +44 (0) 1273 224800
Fax: +44 (0) 1273 770350
email: **mail@ricochet.co.uk**

There is a 'Take Part' page which lists the programmes you can apply for. For job opportunities, go to the 'Jobs' page.

Ricochet in the US

www.ricochettelevision.com

Supernanny; Fat March; The Real Housewives Of New York City; The Alaska Experiment

3800 Barham Boulevard, Suite 210
Los Angeles
CA 90068
Telephone: +1 323 904 4680
Fax: +1 323 904 4681
email: **mail@RicochetTelevision.com**

There is a 'Take Part' link on their website with programmes that are looking for contributors. There is also a 'Jobs' link if you are interested in working for them. 'Due to the nature of TV production,' the website says, 'job opportunities often arise at short notice, so we are happy to take speculative applications from potential production assistants, researchers, production co-ordinators, production managers, APs, producers and directors.'

Email your resume or CV and covering letter, stating your preference for work in Los Angeles to: **resumes@ricochettelevision.com**

Ruggie Media

www.ruggiemedia.com

Extreme Makeover; Nothing But The Truth

14 Fulwood Place
London
C1V 6HZ
Telephone: +44 (0) 207 025 0900
Fax: +44 (0) 207 025 0901
email: **info@ruggiemedia.com**

Scout Productions

www.scoutvision.com

Queer Eye For The Straight Guy/Girl; Knock First; How To Get The Guy; Sox Appeal

6030 Wilshire Blvd, Suite 301
Los Angeles
CA 90036
Telephone: +1 323 933 6030
Fax: +1 323 933 6050

There is a 'Casting' link for the shows that are looking for people to take part.

Sharp Entertainment

www.sharpentertainment.com

Confessions Of A Matchmaker; The Fabulous Life; Kid Protocol; Pants Off, Dance Off

158 West 29th Street, 11th floor
New York
NY 10001
Telephone: +1 212 784 7770
Fax: +1 212 784 7778

Shine Productions

www.shinelimited.com

Gladiators; Masterchef; Project Catwalk; Sex With Mum & Dad; Build A New Life in the Country; Paradise Or Bust

Newcombe House
43–45 Notting Hill Gate
Notting Hill
London
W8 4RT
Telephone: +44 (0) 207 985 7000
Fax: +44 (0) 207 985 7001
email: **info@shinelimited.com**

If they are looking for contributors, they will ask for them on their website. Go to the 'Opportunities' link to find out about programmes that need contributors as well as opportunities to work within the Shine group of companies.

Stick Figure Productions

www.stickfigureproductions.com

Kimora: Life In The Fab Lane; Family Bonds; Amish In The City; The Biz

463 West 45th Street
1st Floor
New York
NY 10036
Telephone: +1 212 277 3600

There is a 'Jobs' link as well as a 'Pitch' link which asks 'Do you
have the perfect project for Stick Figure?'

Stone and Co. Entertainment

www.stoneandcoent.com

*I Propose; The Mole; Shop Til You Drop; Gimme Sugar; Top
Design; Curl Girls; Tim Gunn's Guide To Style*

1040 N Las Palmas Avenue
Building 1
Hollywood
CA 90038
Telephone: +1 323 960 2599
Fax: +1 323 860 3541

Super Delicious Productions

www.superdelicious.net

*The 70s House; Hot Guys Who Cook; MANswers; Farmer
Wants A Wife; Amne$ia; The Assistant*

6121 Santa Monica Blvd
Suite G
Los Angeles
CA 90038
Telephone: +1 323 785 2660
Fax: +1 323 785 2670

Talent Television

www.talenttv.com

Best Of Friends; Skatoony; Test The Nation; No. 1 Soap Fan

Lion House
72–75 Red Lion Street
London
WC1R 4NA
Telephone: +44 (0) 207 421 7800
Fax: +44 (0) 207 421 7811
email: **entertainment@talenttv.com**

There is a 'Contestants' page where you can go to find out if they are looking for people for one of their programmes. There is a 'Jobs' page for information on current vacancies. They do not offer traineeships or work placements.

Talkback Thames

wwtalkbackthames.tv

The X Factor; Dale's Supermarket Sweep; Grand Designs; Property Ladder; Britain's Got Talent; PokerFace; How Clean Is Your House?; The Apprentice; Escape To The Country; Grease Is The Word; Digging Deep

20–21 Newman Street
London
W1T 1PG
Telephone: +44 (0) 207 861 8000
Fax: +44 (0) 207 861 8001

Go to the 'Contact us' page where you can click on the 'Be on tv' link for a list of programmes that are looking for people. The 'Contact us' page also has a links to a Jobs section where any vacancies are advertised. If you would like to send your CV in speculatively, email it to **inspiration@talkbackthames.tv** stating clearly what kind of work you are interested in.

Tiger Aspect Productions

www.tigeraspect.co.uk

Streetmate; Bedroom Diaries; Take It Or Leave It; Vanity Lair

7 Soho Street
London
W1D 3DQ
Telephone: +44 (0) 207 434 6700
Fax: +44 (0) 207 434 1798
email: **general@tigeraspect.co.uk**

Go to the 'Company' page to find a link about jobs with Tiger Aspect.

Trisha TV

www.trishatv.com

Townhouse TV
7 Norwich Business Park
Whiting Road
Norwich
NR4 6DN

Click on the 'Be on the Show' link and fill out the form online and one of the show's producers will get back to you. You can also phone or text (details on the website). There are also details of how to be in the audience as well as information on where coaches, bringing audiences to the studios, will depart from. Seats are limited.

True Entertainment

www.trueentertainment.net

Married Away; Mystery Medicine; Design Star; Mystery Diagnosis; A Baby Story; Whose Wedding Is It Anyway?

601 West 26th Street
Suite 1336
New York
NY 10001
Telephone: +1 212 763 3600
Fax: +1 212 763 3700
email: **mail@trueentertainment.net**

TwentyTwenty

www.twentytwenty.tv

Evacuation; The Sorceror's Apprentice; Bad Lad's Army; Family Brat Camp; Underdogs; I Know What You Ate Last Summer

20 Kentish Town Road
London
NW1 9NX
Telephone: +44 (0) 207 284 2020
Fax: +44 (0) 207 284 1810

They have a 'Be on TV' link on their website to the shows that are looking for people. There is also a 'Jobs' page with details of where to send your CV, depending on which job you are interested in.

Twofour

www.twofourbroadcast.com

Keep It In The Family; Are You Smarter Than A 10 Year Old?; The Hotel Inspector; How To Have Sex After Marriage; Dirty Cows; Learner Driver; Open Gardens; My Great Big Adventure

6–7 St Cross Street
5th floor
London
EC1N 8UA
Telephone: +44 (0) 207 438 1800
Fax: +44 (0) 207 438 1850
email: **enq@twofour.co.uk**

There is a 'Take Part' link which has a description of the programmes looking for contributors and questionnaires and application forms to download. There is a 'Jobs' link with details of which roles the company is recruiting for.

Wall to Wall

www.walltowall.co.uk

1900 House; 1940 House

8–9 Spring Place
Kentish Town
London
NW5 3ER
Telephone: +44 (0) 207 485 7424
Fax: +44 (0) 207 267 5292
email: **mail@walltowall.co.uk**

Go to the 'Contact' page for information on working at the company.

Game shows in the UK

- www.quizzing.co.uk
  A very large quiz site, which lists contestant calls for television and radio.

- www.ukgameshows.com
  Information, trivia, details on all the UK game shows, including those that are looking for contestants.

- A general email for contestant enquiries for BBC-only programmes is: **entertainmentcontestant@bbc.co.uk**

Game shows in the US

- **GSN** (Game Show Network) **www.gsn.com**
  Go to the GSN TV link and you will see the list of shows. Click on the one you are interested in to see if they are looking for contestants or are looking for audiences

- **TV Game Shows** www.tvgameshows.net
  A weekly game show magazine that also advertises casting calls.

Expert contacts

Expert Sources

www.expertsources.co.uk

PO Box 209
Letchworth Garden City
SG6 3ZR
Telephone: +44 (0) 1462 633 884
email: **editor@expertsources.co.uk**

A directory of experts who are available for media interviews and broadcasts.

Foresight News

www.foresightnews.co.uk

The Profile Group (UK) Ltd
Dragon Court 27–29
Macklin Street
London
WC2B 5LX
Telephone: +44 (0) 207 190 7788
Fax: +44 (0) 207 190 7797

Editorial: **hotline@foresightnews.co.uk**
Subscriptions: **sales@foresightnews.co.uk**
General: **info@foresightnews.co.uk**

A website offering a forward planning service giving advance information on thousands of key events over the next few years.

Radio – TV Interview Report

Bradley Communications Corp
135 East Plumstead Ave
PO Box 1206
Lansdowne
PA 19050–8206
Telephone: +1 610 259 0707
Fax: +1 610 284 3704
email: Circ@rtir.com

For free info about advertising as a guest, call 1800 553 8002 ext 408.

Published three times a month, the report is aimed at TV and radio producers in the US and Canada who are looking for authors, spokespersons and experts.

Yearbook of Experts

www.expertclick.com

Editor
Broadcast Interview Source, Inc.
250 Wisconsin Ave NW
Suite 930
Washington, DC 20007–4570
Telephone: +1 202 333 5000

The Yearbook lists expert sources on thousands of topics.

Extras in the UK

NASAA (National Association of Supporting Artiste Agencies)

www.nasaa.org.uk

NASAA is a good source of reputable casting agencies, such as:

- www.2020casting.com
- www.castingcollective.co.uk
- www.guysanddollscasting.com
- www.maddogcasting.com
- www.rayknight.co.uk

Extras in the US

Reputable casting agency sites are:

- www.moviex.com/extras -
- www.centralcasting.org
- www.craigslist.org
- www.twinstalent.tv

Finding an agent

The following are accredited associations for agents with strict codes of conduct for members. You can find a list of agents in the following:

Agents Association

www.agents-uk.com

54 Keyes House
Dolphin Square
London
SW1V 3NA
Telephone: +44 (0) 207 834 0515
Fax: +44 (0) 207 821 0261
email: association@agents-uk.com

National Entertainment Agents Council

www.neac.org.uk

PO Box 112
Seaford
East Sussex
BN25 2DQ
Telephone: +44 (0) 870 755 7612
Fax: +44 (0) 870 755 7613
email: info@neac.org.uk

Association of Talent Agents (ATA)

www.agentassociation.com
9255 Sunset Blvd
Suite 930
Los Angeles
CA 90069
Telephone: +1 310 274 0628
Fax: +1 310 274 5063

A non-profit trade association composed of approximately 100 agency companies engaged in the talent agency business. The membership includes agencies of all sizes representing clients in the motion picture industry, stage, television, radio (including commercials) and literary work.

National Association of Talent Representatives (NATR)

315 West 57th Street
New York
NY 10019
Telephone: +1 212 262 5696
Fax: +1 212 799 6718

Working in broadcasting

Mediabox

www.media-box.co.uk

Telephone: +44 (0) 121 753 4866
email: **info@media-box.co.uk**

Offers grants to 13–19-year-olds, living in England, to make creative media projects.

The Network

www.mgeitf.co.uk/thenetwork/index.asp

Provides free workshops and career advice on working in television to young people aged 18+.

www.hotcourses.com

Directory of college and university courses in Media Production.

Skillset Careers

www.skillset.org

Specialist broadcast careers information and advice service.

Centre for Integration and Improvement of Journalism

www.ciij.org

1600 Holloway Ave
Humanities 307
San Francisco
CA 94132
Telephone: +1 415 338 2083
Fax: + 1 415 338 2084
email: ciij@sfsu.edu

Useful links and resources for journalists and organizations.

Education Video Centre

www.evc.org

120 West 30th Street
7th Floor
New York
NY 10001
Telephone: +1 212 465 9366
Fax: + 212 463 9369
email: info@evc.org

Youth media organization aimed at high-school students and graduates that teaches documentary video skills.

High School Journalism Project

www.hsbj.org

ASNE High School Journalism Initiative
11690B Sunrise Valley Drive
Reston
VA 20191–1409
Telephone: +1 703 453 1135
Fax: +1 703 453 1139

Trains and challenges young people to become the next generation of electronic journalists.

Looking Ahead

www.actorsfund.org

A programme of the Actors' Fund of America which helps young performers and their families deal with the unique issues that come with working in the entertainment industry.

National Endowment for the Arts

www.nea.gov
1100 Pennsylvania Avenue NW
Washington, DC 20506
Telephone: +1 202 682 5400
email: webmgr@arts.endow.gov

An independent federal agency which supports organizations involved in a wide variety of media activity, such as television, film and radio.

Other useful contacts

Ofcom – Office of Communications

www.ofcom.org.uk

Head Office
Riverside House
2a Southwark Bridge Road
London
SE1 9HA
Telephone: +44 (0) 207 981 3000 or 0300 123 3000

Ofcom is the independent regulator and competition authority for the UK communications industries, across television, radio, telecommunications and wireless communications services.

PACT

www.pact.co.uk/

45 Mortimer Street
London
W1W 8HJ
Telephone: +44 (0) 207 331 6000
Fax: +44 (0) 207 331 6700
email (general): enquiries@pact.co.uk
email (orders): publications@pact.co.uk

Gives details on work experience guidelines.

PACT produces an annual directory of indies with all the relevant contact details, as well as projects in development and any specializations.

American Federation of Television and Radio Artists (AFTRA)

www.aftra.org

AFTRA is a national labour union representing over 70,000 performers, journalists and other artists working in the entertainment and news media.

American Women in Radio and Television

www.awrt.org

AWRT National Headquarters
8405 Greensboro Drive
Suite 800
McLean
VA 22102
Telephone: +1 703 506 3290
Fax: +1 703 506 3266

A national, non-profit organization that aims to advance the impact of women in the electronic media, such as television, by educating, advocating and acting as a resource to its members and the industry.

Centre for Media and Public Affairs

www.cmpa.com

2100 L Street, NW
Suite 300
Washington DC 20037
Telephone: +1 202 223 2942
Fax: +1 202 872 4014
email: mail@cmpa.com

The Centre is a non-partisan research and educational organization which conducts scientific studies of the news and entertainment media.

National Association of Broadcasters

www.nab.org

1771 North Street
Washington DC 20036
Telephone: +001 202 429 5300
Fax: +001 202 429 4199
email: **nab@nab.org**

NAB is a trade association that advocates on behalf of local radio and television stations and also broadcast networks before Congress, the Federal Communications Commission and the Courts.

Producers Guild of America (PGA)

www.producersguild.org

8530 Wilshire Boulevard
Suite 450
Beverly Hills
CA 90211
Telephone: +1 310 358 9020
Fax: +1 310 358 9520
email: **info@producersguild.org**

The PGA represents, protects and promotes the interests of all members of the producing team.

Screen Actors Guild

www.sag.org

Hollywood (National Headquarters)
5757 Wilshire Blvd
7th Floor
Los Angeles
CA 90036–3600
Telephone: +1 323 954 1600 (main switchboard)
Telephone: +1 800 SAG 0767 (for SAG Members outside Los Angeles)

New York Division
360 Madison Avenue
12th Floor
New York
NY 10017
Telephone: +1 212 944 1030 (main switchboard)
email: **saginfo@sag.org**

The Guild works to improve and enhance actors' working conditions, compensation and benefits and to be a unified voice on behalf of artists' rights. It represents around 120,000 actors who work in films, TV, commercials, etc. There are 20 SAG branches nationwide.

The Studio System

www.studiosystem.com

A data source for the entertainment industry. Subscribers enjoy unlimited access to detailed information on people, projects, companies engaged in development, production, and performance of film and TV content.

appendix

It will be of no importance in your lifetime or mine.
(Betrand Russell, philosopher, speaking
about television in 1948)

Television – a brief history

How did we get to the point of having reality programmes as
such a major part of the schedules? Are they a new phenomena
or have they been around for years? Where did reality TV
spring from?

Commercial television took off in the States in the early 1940s;
development initially took place on just the east and west
coasts. In Britain, television arrived in 1936, courtesy of the
BBC, where it was the only channel available for 18 years. In
those days, television came in black and white and when you
turned on your television you had to wait for it to warm up.

It was a luxury item; something very few families had. If you
did watch a programme, the chances were that you went to a
friend's house and joined in with the rest of the neighbours to
see it; it was such a very special event. Television really came
of age in Britain in 1953, when an estimated 22 million TV
viewers saw a young Queen Elizabeth crowned, prompting
many people to buy their own sets for the very first time. By
1955, over half of all US households had a television set.

Did you know?

- *Twenty One* was broadcast in the late 1950s. It gained
  notoriety for being a rigged quiz show which nearly caused
  the end of the genre following the United States Senate

investigations. Robert Redford's movie *Quiz Show* (1994) is based on these events.

- *Twenty One* is also known for having the longest break (42 years) between a cancellation and a revived comeback of a television game show on the same network in the history of broadcasting.

While Britain had to make do with one channel for many years, America had a few dozen stations operating by the end of the 1940s. In the early 1950s, the Federal Communications Commission began issuing more broadcasting licenses, which helped stimulate the growth of television around the country.

In the UK, ITV started in 1955, giving the BBC a bit of healthy competition. BBC2 was added in 1964; this is the channel that first broadcast in colour in 1967, with BBC1 following in 1969. By 1979, there were 12 million colour licences in the UK.

The 1950s in America saw a golden age of programming, with such shows as the sitcom *I Love Lucy* (which pioneered the multi-camera shoot for scripted TV), game shows like *Beat The Clock* and talk shows like *The Jack Paar Show*.

Did you know?

- In 1996, BBC1 won 40 per cent of the viewing public when it screened *Only Fools And Horses* at Christmas.
- Reality TV-based programmes count for over 40 per cent of primetime TV in the US – and that figure has been growing each year.

In 1964, Granada Television showed the first in its series *Seven Up!* – interviews with seven-year-olds about their take on ordinary life. Every seven years, the programme followed the lives of the same individuals as they grew up; a strong contender for the first reality series on British television. In 1973, PBS broadcast *An American Family* which showed the Loud family of Santa Barbara, California, going through a divorce. Another reality television highlight came in 1974, with a fly-on-the-wall series for the BBC, called *The Family*, which followed the daily lives of the Wilkins family of Reading. The first in a long line of makeover programmes, *Changing Rooms,* was shown on the BBC for the first time in 1996.

Gradually, more terrestrial channels became available followed by satellite television in the 1980s. More channels and longer schedules meant more content was needed to fill them. Then, in the 1990s, digital television was introduced – an even greater number of channels became available, with more interactivity for viewers.

We now have more channels to choose from than those lucky few television owners in the 1950s could have ever dreamed of. Yes, more channels have meant an increase in repeats (cheaper for the channels) – but still more original programmes are needed to fill the schedules.

Did you know?

- UK channels spent £4.7 billion on programming in 2004 (the most recent figures available).
- Total UK spend on originated programming (excluding news) has grown four per cent per year over the last five years and amounted to £2.6 billion in 2004; these are programmes that are created specifically for, and shown by, the broadcasters.
- UK TV producers made more than 27,000 hours of programmes in 2004 – one of the highest levels of domestically originated content in the world. (Source: Ofcom report 2005)
- Reality production in Los Angeles rose more than 50 per cent in 2006, according to FilmLA, a private, non-profit organization that coordinates location permits. At the same time, feature film production fell 7.4 per cent and commercial production slipped 3.4 per cent.

'There is still a bit of a stigma in this country when you say you work in reality television. There's a kind of eye roll but, whatever people think, they all still watch the programmes. The popularity is there, even amongst the affluent and educated now.'

(Riaz Patel, executive producer of *How To Look Good Naked*, *Ultimates*, *Why Can't I Be You?* and *Into Character*)

Despite seemingly huge sums of money being spent on programming, all channels (and therefore television programmes) are run on a very tight budget. The programme makers have been helped, however, by changes in technology. Whereas before, a producer would need a huge number of cameras and technical staff to make a half-hour programme (which was, therefore, expensive), nowadays that has all changed dramatically. Before, you would have needed a camera operator, sound technician and director at the very least; now presenters can be their own director/cameraman and you can get broadcast quality shots with one hand-held camera.

This throws open lots of possibilities. Why bother creating a soap drama when you can create a docu-soap using real people for a fraction of the cost? Fifteen years ago, in the early 1990s, most ordinary people appearing on television were the subject of a one-hour documentary. Now, with long-running docu-soaps (which can run for eight, ten, even 20 programmes), a contributor can be on screen for weeks. *Big Brother*, for example, runs for around 14 weeks; that is a quarter of the year.

So, with each new development in television, the rise of multi-channels and the introduction of new technology, there are more hours of the schedules to fill. From the programme makers' point of view, one endless resource is the public, ordinary people in other words. And whilst some critics will complain that television programmes are all the same now, the producers will argue that new people can make 'old' subjects fresh again.

> *Colour television! Bah, I won't believe it until I see it in black and white.*
>
> (Samuel Goldwyn, Hollywood producer)

Did you know?

Thixendale, a village in the Yorkshire Wolds, was unable to receive a clear TV signal right up until the late 1990s thanks to the local geography. The villagers raised £8000 to get a communal transmitter and 39 individual aerials that allowed residents to receive blizzard-free, clear pictures on terrestrial television for the first time in June 1997.

How television programmes are developed and sold

In the US ...

In the States, there is no national broadcasting service (like the BBC). Local markets have their own television stations which are either affiliated to or owned and operated by a TV network (such as Fox or CBS). Usually, a station affiliated to a particular network will not show programmes from rival networks.

However, to ensure local presences in television broadcasting, federal law restricts the amount of network programming local stations can run. Right up to the 1980s, local stations supplemented network programming with their own shows. Today, it is more likely that stations will only produce local news shows. The rest of their schedule is made up of syndicated shows, or material produced independently and sold to individual stations in the local market.

The 1970s saw the appearance of national networks dedicated exclusively to cable broadcasting (such as E! Entertainment, Oxygen, the Food Network, Bravo, Lifetime, HGTV, A&E). Today, most American households receive cable TV, and cable networks collectively have greater viewership than broadcast networks.

All the networks have development departments (or 'alternative' programming as they are sometimes called). These departments will go out to producers like Mark Burnett, Magical Elves or Bunim-Murray and find projects that they may buy (or run as a pilot) before possibly making into a series.

In the UK ...

Some broadcasters and networks (such as the BBC and MTV) have in-house development and production departments, responsible for conceiving and making some of the programmes shown on those channels. These broadcasters also commission independent companies (such as Shine, Twofour and Endemol) to make programmes for them. Other channels, such as Channel 4 and Five, depend entirely on shows commissioned from independent companies.

Most independent companies have dedicated development departments whose job it is to come up with ideas for programmes and persuade the various broadcasters to commission them to make those programmes. At any given moment, they will know what type of programmes their client broadcasters are looking for.

How it works

There may be a few local differences depending on whether you are sitting in Los Angeles or London but the next stages are fairly similar for either country.

For their part, the broadcasters and networks let the production companies know what they are looking for in one of several ways:

- information on the producer's or commissioning section of their website (for example, **www.bbc.co.uk/commissioning**)
- briefing sessions held by commissioning editors/development departments for a number of independent companies
- one-to-one meetings between someone from the company and one of the broadcaster's commissioning editors.

The development team's job is to respond to what the channels are looking for and come up with ideas for each client (the broadcaster) that meets its current needs. That can be easier said than done because those needs change constantly and rapidly. Sometimes, commissioning editors will be very specific with their requests (for example, 'We need a series about children and gardening or businesses and dogs'); at other times, they are much more general ('We need programmes that appeal to young men ... or middle-aged housewives ... or both') and sometimes, they are very, very general ('We need innovative, funny and intelligent programmes').

Having said that, some of the best television ideas have been ones that have not come about as a result of a specific brief from a channel or network; they are just a very good idea. Part of the development team's expertise is knowing how to pitch that very good idea by understanding the details (the format of the programme, the tone and style, which presenter to use, what kind of people to cast and so on) and which channel to pitch it to.

Once a company or department comes up with an idea, they will pitch it in one of several ways:

- Send a brief email to a commissioning editor, with two or three lines that sketch the basic concept of the show. This works when they know the commissioning editor well and work with them often. If they know each other, there is more chance of that editor opening the email, reading it and understanding how they would make the programme.
- Send a longer proposal – one or two sides of A4 paper giving more detail. At some point, the two or three lines of a proposal are going to have to be expanded into a longer proposal which will then act as a blueprint for making the programme
- Pitch the idea verbally at a meeting with a commissioning editor.

However the first approach is made, the chances are that weeks and months of discussions, meetings and rewrites will follow before the show is commissioned ... if it is commissioned at all. One development executive calculated roughly that his company pitches around 20 ideas for every seven or eight that interests a commissioning editor – of which only one will actually get the go-ahead.

During this period, everything about the programme comes under scrutiny: how will the show work, what is the budget, who will direct the programme and so on. The time can often be extended even further if the commissioning editor, with whom the production company are working, has a boss who he or she has to convince that this particular idea is a good one; who, in turn, might also have a boss to persuade. It can be a long and tortuous process.

Finally, the channel will commit to the programme and give it the green light. Alternatively, they may decide to commit to a period of funded development. This is where they give the production company a few thousand pounds/dollars to: conduct in-depth research; and/or to do some test filming; and/or to secure access (in the case of a documentary); and/or find a presenter; and/or produce a really long written document describing the programme in detail.

With a series, the broadcaster might commission a pilot before they make a decision about the series – a one-off episode. Sometimes these are cheap and not for broadcast; other times, they involve a lot of money and will go out on the television. Either way, the final decision about the series will depend on the success of the pilot. If broadcast, its popularity with viewers will be the major deciding factor as to whether a complete series is commissioned.

index

teach® yourself

From Advanced Sudoku to Zulu, you'll find everything you need in the **teach yourself** range, in books, on CD and on DVD.

Visit **www.teachyourself.co.uk** for more details.

Advanced Sudoku and Kakuro
Afrikaans
Alexander Technique
Algebra
Ancient Greek
Applied Psychology
Arabic
Arabic Conversation
Aromatherapy
Art History
Astrology
Astronomy
AutoCAD 2004
AutoCAD 2007
Ayurveda
Baby Massage and Yoga
Baby Signing
Baby Sleep
Bach Flower Remedies
Backgammon
Ballroom Dancing
Basic Accounting
Basic Computer Skills
Basic Mathematics
Beauty
Beekeeping
Beginner's Arabic Script
Beginner's Chinese Script
Beginner's Dutch

Beginner's French
Beginner's German
Beginner's Greek
Beginner's Greek Script
Beginner's Hindi
Beginner's Hindi Script
Beginner's Italian
Beginner's Japanese
Beginner's Japanese Script
Beginner's Latin
Beginner's Mandarin Chinese
Beginner's Portuguese
Beginner's Russian
Beginner's Russian Script
Beginner's Spanish
Beginner's Turkish
Beginner's Urdu Script
Bengali
Better Bridge
Better Chess
Better Driving
Better Handwriting
Biblical Hebrew
Biology
Birdwatching
Blogging
Body Language
Book Keeping
Brazilian Portuguese

German Grammar
German Phrasebook
German Starter Kit
German Vocabulary
Globalization
Go
Golf
Good Study Skills
Great Sex
Green Parenting
Greek
Greek Conversation
Greek Phrasebook
Growing Your Business
Guitar
Gulf Arabic
Hand Reflexology
Hausa
Herbal Medicine
Hieroglyphics
Hindi
Hindi Conversation
Hinduism
History of Ireland, The
Home PC Maintenance and
  Networking
How to DJ
How to Run a Marathon
How to Win at Casino Games
How to Win at Horse Racing
How to Win at Online Gambling
How to Win at Poker
How to Write a Blockbuster
Human Anatomy & Physiology
Hungarian
Icelandic
Improve Your French
Improve Your German
Improve Your Italian
Improve Your Spanish
Improving Your Employability
Indian Head Massage
Indonesian
Instant French
Instant German
Instant Greek
Instant Italian

Instant Japanese
Instant Portuguese
Instant Russian
Instant Spanish
Internet, The
Irish
Irish Conversation
Irish Grammar
Islam
Israeli-Palestinian Conflict, The
Italian
Italian Conversation
Italian for Homebuyers
Italian Grammar
Italian Phrasebook
Italian Starter Kit
Italian Verbs
Italian Vocabulary
Japanese
Japanese Conversation
Java
JavaScript
Jazz
Jewellery Making
Judaism
Jung
Kama Sutra, The
Keeping Aquarium Fish
Keeping Pigs
Keeping Poultry
Keeping a Rabbit
Knitting
Korean
Latin
Latin American Spanish
Latin Dictionary
Latin Grammar
Letter Writing Skills
Life at 50: For Men
Life at 50: For Women
Life Coaching
Linguistics
LINUX
Lithuanian
Magic
Mahjong
Malay

Managing Stress
Managing Your Own Career
Mandarin Chinese
Mandarin Chinese Conversation
Marketing
Marx
Massage
Mathematics
Meditation
Middle East Since 1945, The
Modern China
Modern Hebrew
Modern Persian
Mosaics
Music Theory
Mussolini's Italy
Nazi Germany
Negotiating
Nepali
New Testament Greek
NLP
Norwegian
Norwegian Conversation
Old English
One-Day French
One-Day French – the DVD
One-Day German
One-Day Greek
One-Day Italian
One-Day Polish
One-Day Portuguese
One-Day Spanish
One-Day Spanish – the DVD
One-Day Turkish
Origami
Owning a Cat
Owning a Horse
Panjabi
PC Networking for Small
  Businesses
Personal Safety and Self
  Defence
Philosophy
Philosophy of Mind
Philosophy of Religion
Phone French
Phone German

Phone Italian
Phone Japanese
Phone Mandarin Chinese
Phone Spanish
Photography
Photoshop
PHP with MySQL
Physics
Piano
Pilates
Planning Your Wedding
Polish
Polish Conversation
Politics
Portuguese
Portuguese Conversation
Portuguese for Homebuyers
Portuguese Grammar
Portuguese Phrasebook
Postmodernism
Pottery
PowerPoint 2003
PR
Project Management
Psychology
Quick Fix French Grammar
Quick Fix German Grammar
Quick Fix Italian Grammar
Quick Fix Spanish Grammar
Quick Fix: Access 2002
Quick Fix: Excel 2000
Quick Fix: Excel 2002
Quick Fix: HTML
Quick Fix: Windows XP
Quick Fix: Word
Quilting
Recruitment
Reflexology
Reiki
Relaxation
Retaining Staff
Romanian
Running Your Own Business
Russian
Russian Conversation
Russian Grammar
Sage Line 50

Sanskrit
Screenwriting
Second World War, The
Serbian
Setting Up a Small Business
Shorthand Pitman 2000
Sikhism
Singing
Slovene
Small Business Accounting
Small Business Health Check
Songwriting
Spanish
Spanish Conversation
Spanish Dictionary
Spanish for Homebuyers
Spanish Grammar
Spanish Phrasebook
Spanish Starter Kit
Spanish Verbs
Spanish Vocabulary
Speaking On Special Occasions
Speed Reading
Stalin's Russia
Stand Up Comedy
Statistics
Stop Smoking
Sudoku
Swahili
Swahili Dictionary
Swedish
Swedish Conversation
Tagalog
Tai Chi
Tantric Sex
Tap Dancing
Teaching English as a Foreign
    Language
Teams & Team Working
Thai
Thai Conversation
Theatre
Time Management
Tracing Your Family History
Training
Travel Writing
Trigonometry

Turkish
Turkish Conversation
Twentieth Century USA
Typing
Ukrainian
Understanding Tax for Small
    Businesses
Understanding Terrorism
Urdu
Vietnamese
Visual Basic
Volcanoes, Earthquakes and
    Tsunamis
Watercolour Painting
Weight Control through Diet &
    Exercise
Welsh
Welsh Conversation
Welsh Dictionary
Welsh Grammar
Wills & Probate
Windows XP
Wine Tasting
Winning at Job Interviews
Word 2003
World Faiths
Writing Crime Fiction
Writing for Children
Writing for Magazines
Writing a Novel
Writing a Play
Writing Poetry
Xhosa
Yiddish
Yoga
Your Wedding
Zen
Zulu